I Was That Masked Man

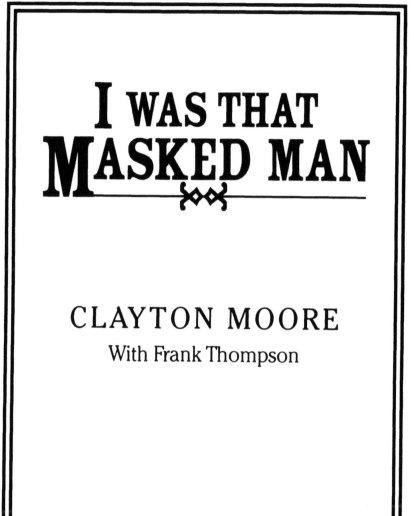

I WAS THAT
MASKED MAN

CLAYTON MOORE
With Frank Thompson

TAYLOR TRADE PUBLISHING

Lanham • New York • Dallas • Boulder• Toronto • Oxford

TAYLOR TRADE PUBLISHING
An Imprint of the Rowman & Littlefield Publishing Group
4501 Forbes Boulevard, Suite 200
Lanham, MD 20706

Library of Congress Cataloging-in-Publication Data

Moore, Clayton, 1914–
 I was that masked man / Clayton Moore with Frank Thompson.
  p.   cm.
 Filmography: p.243
 Includes index.
 ISBN 978-0-87833-216-8

 1. Moore, Clayton, 1914– . 2. Actors—United States—Biography.
I. Thompson, Frank T., 1952– . II. Title.
PN2287.M6948A3   1996
791.45'028'092—dc20
 [B]   96-2889
                                                         CIP

Table of Contents

Foreword by Leonard Maltin   ix

Preface by Frank Thompson   xi

Introduction by Frank Thompson   1

1 Birth of a Ranger   13

2 A Cowboy Actor in the Big Apple   35

3 Hollywood!   43

4 Republic Pictures   61

5 In the Army Now   71

6 King of the B's   79

7 Hi Yo Silver, Awayyy!   111

8 Back to the Big Screen   131

9 Jay Silverheels   143

10 The Lone Ranger Rides Again!   151

11 England and a New Daughter   185

12 Adventures on Television   195

13 You Don't Pull the Mask Off the
   Ol' Lone Ranger   203

14 The Adventures of Clayton Moore   221

15 Who is That Masked Man?   231

   Appendix   243

   Index   257

Acknowledgments

Grateful thanks go to those who helped make this book possible: Dawn Moore, Clarita Moore, Michael Gerrity, Kate Seago, Ann Marie Tierney, Leonard Maltin, Claire McCulloch Thompson, Rand Brooks, Dave Holland, David Rothel, Susan Grode, Jim Hoiby, Broadway Video, Mike Emmerich, Frank Weimann, Thel Arthur, and, of course, Sally Allen Moore.

A fiery horse with the speed of light, a cloud of dust and a hearty "Hi Yo Silver!" The Lone Ranger rides again. With his faithful Indian companion Tonto, the daring and resourceful masked rider of the plains led the fight for law and order in the early western United States. Return with us now to those thrilling days of yesteryear. Out of the past come the thundering hoofbeats of the great horse Silver. The Lone Ranger rides again!

Foreword

Like millions of other kids of my generation, I grew up believing Clayton Moore *was* the Lone Ranger. It wasn't just that he gave a good performance as the masked rider; he seemed to embody the spirit and essence of the character. There was, in fact, no evidence of "acting."

It was many years later that I met Clayton at a fan convention in New York City. He was scheduled to sign autographs for a set amount of time one afternoon, but the line was long and he didn't want to disappoint anyone. After staying past his scheduled period, he was leaving the room when a father and son rushed up to ask if he would pose for a photograph. He smiled and said yes, then not only posed, but posed *in character!*

Right then and there I knew he was someone special.

I've been with Clayton a number of times since then, and he's never let me down or caused me to change my high opinion of him. He recognizes that many of us (especially those of us who grew up watching him in the 1950s) regard him with a kind of reverence. And far from being put off by this blur between his television persona and his private self, he seems to thrive on it.

No one could be as consistently noble as the Lone Ranger. Few would even try. But Clayton Moore has made an honest effort to carry himself like the hero he is to so many millions of fans. At the annual Golden Boot Awards ceremony, where veterans of television and movie Westerns are honored, Roy Rogers, Gene Autry, and Dale Evans are cheered with great enthusiasm. But consistently, the biggest ovation of the evening goes to Clayton Moore whenever he recites "The Lone Ranger Creed." He brings the house down every time.

This charming autobiography tells us more than any of us have ever known about the man behind the mask; he emerges as a likable, hard-working actor who enjoyed his job. It's a treat to get to know Clayton Moore as someone other than the fabled crusader for law and order, and we're all in his debt for sharing these memories on paper.

Clayton Moore may not be larger than life, like the Lone Ranger, but he is a genuinely good man—and there aren't enough of them in this world. If you ask me, he *is* a hero. God bless him.

LEONARD MALTIN

Preface

The image is burned into the imaginations of several generations. Into a stark landscape of craggy rock gallops a brilliant white stallion. On his back is a figure in blue suit, white hat, and black mask, mysterious and mythic at the same time. Pausing at the summit of an incline, the stallion rears magnificently, pawing the air with his front hooves. As the stirring, trumpeting strains of Rossini's *William Tell* Overture fill the soundtrack, the Masked Man calls out, "Hi Yo Silver! Awayyy!" And off they ride, into adventure, into legend.

A breathless announcer tells us who it is. But who doesn't already know? He's the Lone Ranger, the champion of good, the bane of the outlaw, and these are the opening moments of the television show that broadcast his adventures from 1949–1957—and on into the future.

With his faithful Indian friend Tonto and his mighty horse Silver, the Lone Ranger was a genuine hero, equal to any task. Through his many dramatic adventures, spanning over six decades, on radio, television, and in the movies, the Lone Ranger has become more than just a memorable fictional character. He is the epitome of a particular kind of American archetype: brave, honest, compassionate, patriotic, inventive—an unswerving champion of justice and fair play.

Many actors have portrayed the Lone Ranger over the years, from Brace Beemer on the radio to Klinton Spilsbury in the ill-fated 1981 motion picture *The Legend of the Lone Ranger*. But one man has become synonymous with the role—

Clayton Moore.

Adults in their forties and fifties have only to hear his voice to become ten years old again. Children who weren't even born when *The Lone Ranger* was on the air in the fifties flock to him at personal appearances. Audiences' fascination with the Lone Ranger and Clayton Moore has never died out. Over the years, he has been asked countless times to tell his own story, and now he has, reliving for his legions of fans those thrilling days of his personal yesteryear.

Although Clayton Moore became famous for his portrayal of the Lone Ranger, that character is only one aspect of Moore's remarkable life and career. By the time he won the role in 1949, he had already lived a life worthy of a Republic serial, filled with adventure and glamour, danger and hardship. He was an athlete, a trapeze artist, a model, and a soldier. But from earliest childhood there was really only one thing Clayton Moore wanted to become: a movie cowboy hero. His wish came true, first in exciting, low-budget cliffhangers like *Jesse James Rides Again* (1947) and then as the star of the television series *The Lone Ranger*.

Clayton Moore's story is an exciting and nostalgic tour of Hollywood in the Golden Age—table hopping at glamorous nightspots like the Trocadero with "Mexican Spitfire" Lupe Velez, lounging beside Cary Grant's pool, and creating indelible movie moments at studios like Warner Bros., MGM, and Republic. Through him we experience the fast-paced world of the serial, the excitement (and agony) of turning out several half-hour television episodes a week, and the good-natured camaraderie of actors, directors, stuntmen, and crews on distant locations.

But his is also a story about change. When Clayton Moore began portraying the Lone Ranger, it was a role he coveted. But it was only that—a role. A decade later, it was much, much more. The two identities had merged until only Moore's family and closest friends could recognize the line that separated them. It's a remarkable transformation; Moore was inspired by the honesty, integrity, and idealism inherent in the Lone Ranger and wanted to embody those traits himself. Despite the distinct disadvantage of being a real person and not a fictional character, he has succeeded in doing just that. There are no skeletons in Clayton Moore's closet. He is exactly what he appears to be—moral, upstanding, generous, honest, and patriotic.

In the seventies and eighties, new film versions of classic characters from popular culture were produced: Superman, Batman, Tarzan, Dick Tracy, Popeye, and many others. Some of these figures had long been identified with one actor or another. These new film twists on old favorites may have disgruntled a fan or two, but they inspired nothing like the cry of dismay that arose when someone dared to suggest that Clayton Moore was not the real Lone Ranger.

When the Wrather Corporation announced in 1979 that they were going to produce a new film, *The Legend of the Lone Ranger*, a restraining order prevented Clayton Moore from wearing the black mask and appearing in character. The Wrather Corporation felt it was time that a new, young Lone Ranger took over. Clayton Moore disagreed. Since he had been making his living from personal appearances as the Lone Ranger since the midfifties, he was upset by the order and fought back. So did his fans: their uproar was immediate and tremendous. Petitions were circulated, garnering over a million signatures. Moore received over 400,000 letters of support. The Wrather Corporation received who knows how many angry letters of complaint.

After *The Legend of the Lone Ranger* died a terrible death at the box office, the restraining order was quietly dropped. The mask was returned to Clayton Moore. It was official. There have been many actors who have played the Lone Ranger. But only one of them *became* the Lone Ranger. The whole world knows who that is.

Working with Clayton Moore on this book has not only been rewarding, it has been inspiring. For a guy who wears a mask, he is uncommonly open and unguarded. He truly believes in the positive attributes of the role he plays and embodies them truly and fully. Cynics want to believe that it's all just an act, that those who project decency and honor publicly must be just the opposite when the shades are drawn. But everyone who meets Clayton Moore comes away knowing that this is the genuine article. He played a hero on television. And, by sheer force of will, he became one in real life.

FRANK THOMPSON

INTRODUCTION

The Story of the Lone Ranger

Although we now celebrate Clayton Moore's status as the one and only Kimo Sabe, several actors have played the part on radio, television, motion pictures, and the stage. So many, in fact, that we don't even know who all of them were. Even though the character is called the *Lone* Ranger, he has plenty of other Lone Rangers to keep him company.

Clayton Moore is the most famous one, of course. And radio's Brace Beemer was idolized by the public during his nearly fourteen years of playing the role. And Robert Livingston and Lee Powell played the Lone Ranger in those fast-paced Republic serials of the thirties.

But who was that *first* masked man?

To answer that question, we must go back to those not-so-thrilling days of yesteryear—1929, a year that saw the United States plunged into the most devastating economic depression in the nation's history. Life was tough for nearly everybody in 1929, but an enterprising businessman named George Washington Trendle chose this dark period to expand his personal empire. Trendle was a motion picture distributor, but he had become interested in the growing influence of radio, a medium that Trendle felt was filled with economic potential. He and his partners bought WXYZ ("The last word in radio!"), a little 1,000 watt station in Detroit, Michigan, and immediately began making plans to dominate broadcasting throughout North America.

WXYZ made its mark on the listening public with cops-and-robbers melodramas like *Manhunters* and domestic comedies such as *Hank and Honey*. Some of the station's best programs were written by the prolific Fran Striker, who lived in Buffalo, New York. Striker was both fast and good; he churned out scripts at an exhausting pace, always working on several radio serials at once.

When Trendle first had the idea that would eventually turn into *The Lone Ranger*, he turned to Striker; they are generally regarded as the fathers of the Lone Ranger. But laying all the credit at either Trendle's or Striker's feet for this momentous creation is a bit simplistic. As Western historian Dave Holland correctly points out, *The Lone Ranger* wasn't created in one explosive moment—it evolved gradually, through the contributions of any number of people. In some ways, the character and the legend have never stopped evolving.

Fran Striker was first contacted about helping to create a Western series for Trendle in 1932, but by the time he came aboard, Trendle and his staff had already been tossing around ideas for several months. Trendle was interested in developing a Western because he knew it would appeal to kids and he had a keen eye for the extra income that was possible through radio premiums, toys, and souvenirs. *Because* the series would be aimed at young people, Trendle insisted that the shows contain only clean and wholesome stories and dialogue. His hero would be pure, upstanding, strong, fair, patriotic and kind, but a bit mysterious, too—a bit of Robin Hood mixed with a dash of Zorro.

In creative sessions, concepts for the new serial were batted around by Trendle and the rest of the WXYZ staff. Ideas came from everyone and everywhere. Someone suggested giving him a brilliant white horse. Someone else suggested naming the horse Silver—just like cowboy star Buck Jones's horse. Trendle wanted his hero to wear a mask and thought that he might be a former Texas Ranger. Little by little, more details were added, including silver bullets and a shout filled with hearty laughter: "Hi Yi Ha Ha Ha!"

Fran Striker rummaged through his trunk of scripts— both produced and unproduced—and decided to adapt one of his earlier series, *Covered Wagon Days*; in fact, for a short time, this was the working title of the new series, too.

The WXYZ dramatic director, Jim Jewell, wrote to Striker early on instructing him to infuse his scripts with "all the hokum of the masked rider, rustlers, Killer Pete, heroine on the train tracks, fight on top of box cars, Indian badman, two-gun bank robbers, etc."

Striker took these suggestions and ran with them. Little by little, *The Lone Ranger* was taking shape. Not all of Striker's contributions, however, were inspired. He suggested the balmy "Beyond the Blue Horizon" as the show's theme song. And his hero really was a *lone* ranger, working all by himself. Jewell wrote to Striker on February 15, 1933, "It might be a good idea also [to give the Lone Ranger a sidekick], an Indian half-breed who always stands ready at his command to help him...." Striker responded with a wise old half-breed named Tonto. While The Lone Ranger remained essentially an ageless character over the years, Tonto actually grew *younger*, stronger and more virile—and over time he became a full-blooded Indian. Throughout the entire run of the radio show, from 1933 to 1954, Tonto was played by one man, a former Shakespearean actor named John Todd.

Striker's original Lone Ranger was also quite violent; in the first submitted script he shot seven bad guys "clean through the forehead." Trendle nipped the Ranger's violent streak in the bud. He wanted a moral, upright hero, one who would never shoot to kill, but only to wound or disarm. He told Striker to refine the character until the Lone Ranger stood for everything good and decent in the West. That first bloody script never made it to the air.

It is generally accepted that the first radio episode of *The Lone Ranger* aired on January 30, 1933. Dave Holland, in his exceptional book, *From Out of the Past: A Pictorial History of the Lone Ranger*, has discovered that the real first air date was February 2, although Trendle had broadcast a sort of dress rehearsal a few nights earlier. Regardless of the date, the first adventure of the Lone Ranger immediately thrilled and captivated its audience. It opened with a bang. Someone had a better idea about the theme music than Striker's "Beyond the Blue Horizon." Instead, the show crashed onto the airwaves with the trumpeting strains of Rossini's *William Tell* Overture, music which had been chosen for its exciting "galloping" quality. Then, announcer Fred Foy spoke those memorable words—

"A fiery horse, with a speed of light, a cloud of dust, a hearty laugh—the Lone Ranger!"

And the masked rider was off on a long, long ride into legend.

Of course, the "hearty laugh" didn't quite hit the nail on the head. It soon became refined into "Hi Yo Silver! Away!" which, Trendle felt, had kind of a nice ring to it.

But, to get back to our original question, who was that *first* masked man on that first episode?

He was George Stenius, a twenty-two-year-old actor who had recently returned to Detroit after traveling with a theatrical production of *Elizabeth the Queen*. Although he had a distinctive voice and was an expressive performer, Stenius was much more interested in writing. After staying with the show briefly, he decided to return to New York to concentrate on writing plays. Once there, he decided that motion pictures offered even more rewarding writing opportunities, so on August 23, 1933, he headed for Hollywood. There, having changed his name to George Seaton, he wrote scripts for films like the Marx Brothers' *A Day at the Races* (1938); *Charley's Aunt* (1941), starring Jack Benny; and *The Song of Bernadette* (1943), starring Jennifer Jones. In the midforties, Seaton began directing his own scripts, winning Academy Awards for his screenplays for *Miracle on 34th Street* (1947) and *The Country Girl* (1955), both of which he also directed.

Throughout this distinguished career, Seaton always maintained a soft spot in his heart for the brief period when he was that masked man, laughing fondly at the primitive conditions under which the shows were produced. "At that time there were no union rules," he told *Lone Ranger* historian David Rothel. "Consequently, we didn't have any sound effects men. All of us in the cast had to do our own sound effects, with a script in one hand and paraphernalia in the other." A versatile actor, Seaton usually played multiple roles besides that of the Lone Ranger.

Jack Deeds was the next actor to don the mask, but he only wore it a scant two days. Annoyed listeners complained that Deeds didn't sound anything like a cowboy, so he was promptly replaced by a Wayne University drama student named Earle Graser.

Graser was the first actor who really clicked with the public as *the* Lone Ranger. Every kid in America knew his voice. And why not? He played the part three times a week for seven years. He didn't look much like the Lone Ranger, though; Graser was rather small, unathletic, and unprepossessing. But vocally, he was perfect. So perfect, in fact, that a recording of Graser shouting "Hi Yo Silver! Away!" was used for years on both the radio and television *Lone Ranger* episodes.

By the midthirties, *The Lone Ranger* was a phenomenon, popular not only on the radio but also for books (and comic books), toys, radio premiums, the Sunday funnies. Actors in masks (usually a WXYZ manager named Brace Beemer) were sent out to do vaudeville turns as the Lone Ranger and to make public appearances at schools, in parades, at fairgrounds, and numerous other occasions. With all this hoopla, it became inevitable that Hollywood would come calling.

Republic Pictures was a leading producer of B-Westerns and adventure serials. Beginning in the midthirties the studio had already released such popular chapter-plays as *The Vigilantes Are Coming* (1936), *Dick Tracy* (1937), *The Painted Stallion* (1937), *Zorro Rides Again* (1937) and several others. Nearly every studio in Hollywood made serials, but Republic quickly established itself as a leader in the field. The studio also released popular and profitable B-Westerns with such enduring stars as John Wayne, Roy Rogers, and Gene Autry.

Republic head Herbert Yates knew that there was gold in "that thar" mask and approached Trendle with the idea of making a *Lone Ranger* feature film. At first they thought it would be perfect for the studio's biggest cowboy star, Gene Autry, but cooler heads prevailed and it was decided to build a serial around the character (although the idea of a singing Lone Ranger *is* kind of intriguing).

The Lone Ranger was released as a fifteen-chapter serial in 1937, starring Lee Powell as the ranger and Chief Thundercloud as Tonto, and directed by Republic's young turks William Witney and John English. Of all subsequent retellings of the Lone Ranger's adventures, this first serial deviates most seriously from the accepted story elements. *The Lone Ranger* is a whodunit featuring five Texas Rangers, all of similar type and build, any one of whom could be the Lone Ranger. One by one they are killed off until only one is left.

The mystery is deepened by a slightly underhanded trick: veteran voice actor Billy Bletcher, heard in countless Walt Disney animated films like *The Three Little Pigs* (1933) and *Snow White and the Seven Dwarfs* (1937), was brought in to dub the voice of the ranger whenever the mask was on. "Engaging someone to do this [dubbing] was a bit surprising since the film had already been made," Bletcher later said, "but the man who had been photographed didn't sound anything like the voice that so many children and grownups were accustomed to hearing. We had to lip-match everything he said and put the voice into the image of the actor seen on the screen." In addition to this vocal switcheroo, the Rangers' masks covered the entire face, making identification even more difficult. Viewers didn't learn until the final chapter which Lone Ranger was the real one.

In 1939 Republic produced *The Lone Ranger Rides Again*, another fifteen-chapter serial. In this one, the masked man is played by Robert Livingston, already popular as one

never sign his own name when asked for an autograph. He always had to wear the mask when appearing in public, and "public" was defined as a group of three or more people. Beemer seemed to have no problem with these restrictions. He played the part to the hilt, acquiring fifteen custom-made costumes, six pairs of hand-tooled boots, six special white Stetson hats, and a hand-carved saddle valued at three thousand dollars. An expert horseman, he rode his own horse, Silver's Pride, when making personal appearances.

Just as Clayton Moore would do in later years, Beemer made it a point to incorporate the ideals of the Lone Ranger into his personal life. Announcer Fred Foy called Beemer, "the Lone Ranger, whether on the microphone or off. I know it was one of his prime purposes to visit children's hospitals where many youngsters, of course, idolized The Lone Ranger. This was to them a real-life hero, and there were many instances where in just going in in his full regalia as The Lone Ranger, the mask and so on, that this would give the youngsters a tremendous lift."

Clayton Moore and Jay Silverheels assumed the roles of the Lone Ranger and Tonto for Trendle's television show which began in 1949. But even while Moore was reshaping the masked man in his own image, Brace Beemer was still upholding the tradition on the radio. For those five years there were *two* Lone Rangers (well, three, counting the year that John Hart took over on television). *Lone Ranger* fans didn't seem to be confused by the dueling rangers, even when Jay Silverheels went out on personal appearances with Brace Beemer!

The Lone Ranger became more popular year after year, so one has to wonder why it took so long for the character to reach the screen in a feature film. Trendle was apparently so unhappy with the liberties taken by Republic in the two serials that he vowed not to let anyone make another *Lone Ranger* film over which he could not have total control. In 1939 Universal approached him with the idea of doing a third serial, but the project went nowhere. Republic reedited the first serial into an ersatz feature, *Hi Yo Silver*, which it released in 1940, but a true *Lone Ranger* feature was not produced until after Jack Wrather took over the character in 1954.

The Lone Ranger (1956) and *The Lone Ranger and the Lost City of Gold* (1958), both of which starred Moore and Silverheels, were exciting Westerns filled with action, which played out like more expensive, elaborate versions of the television show. Audiences flocked to both of them, although the critics weren't always so enthusiastic. Today the first feature seems far better than the second; film historian Phil Hardy called it, "a masterpiece of children's cinema" but thought *Lost City of Gold* was "a lackluster sequel."

Very few critics or audience members thought too highly—then or now—of the next *Lone Ranger* feature: William A. Fraker's *The Legend of the Lone Ranger* (1981). Although Clayton Moore thought the best idea for a feature film would be to have an aging Lone Ranger pass on the mask to a younger man, *Legend* started all over with the origin of the character: the ambush of the Texas Rangers, the meeting of the Lone Ranger and Tonto, and so forth. Fraker, an award-winning cinematographer (*Rosemary's Baby* [1968], *Bullitt* [1968], *One Flew Over the Cuckoo's Nest* [1975], and many more) had directed a fine Western, *Monte Walsh*, in 1970 and was the perfect choice to helm this exercise in Hollywood mythmaking. Fraker brought to *The Legend of the Lone Ranger* a keen eye for composition and a gift for capturing sweeping action and beautiful vistas on film. But the movie was marred by an abrupt story line and some less than brilliant performances. It was by no means the disaster that many have made it out to be—although many of Clayton Moore's fans were so outraged at his shabby treatment by the Wrather Corporation that they didn't much care whether the movie was any good or not.

However, to longtime *Lone Ranger* fans, *The Legend of the Lone Ranger* did include one nostalgic moment—and almost included another. Veteran *Lone Ranger* announcer Fred Foy was cast in a brief part as the mayor of Del Rio. Unfortunately, his role ended up on the cutting room floor. (However, Foy's voice is heard at the end of the film.) John Hart, who played the ranger on television during the 1953 season, was luckier than Foy. He made it into the picture with the small but crucial role of a crusading newspaper editor.

No one really knows exactly how many actors have portrayed the Lone Ranger on radio and television, in the movies and on stage. But one thing is certain—there will be others. The mysterious and valiant masked man, with his brave and faithful companion Tonto, have thrilled countless millions of people over the past six decades. There is no reason to think that the pair won't be back again, with a fiery steed, a cloud of dust and a hearty "Hi Yo Silver!" all the way into the twenty-first century.

CHAPTER ONE

Birth of a Ranger

Near Iverson's Ranch, in Chatsworth, California, a few miles north of Los Angeles, stands a magnificent formation of craggy stone. Almost every American kid who watched television in the 1950s and 1960s can recognize it immediately: Lone Ranger Rock. My horse Silver rears up before it, with me on his back, in the title sequence of every episode of *The Lone Ranger*. It used to be wild, beautiful country up at Iverson's where we filmed the location scenes for so many of those shows. It's a lot more tame now. Lone Ranger Rock is surrounded by modern condominiums. A major freeway roars past it. The city is claiming this remote place, slowly but surely.

Yet Lone Ranger Rock is still there, just as straight and tall and imposing as in those "thrilling days of yesteryear." Things have changed in other ways, too, in the five decades since I first laid eyes on the rock. Kids nowadays aren't so quick to worship heroes. The world is a lot more complicated; we don't seem to believe in absolute good and evil—white hats and black hats—anymore. It's fashionable to think of virtue and honor and bravery as naive, outmoded emotions.

But deep down, I believe that people still cling to those ideals. When I first appeared on television as the Lone Ranger, Jay Silverheels (Tonto) and I used to do a lot of public appearances. Years earlier, when George W. Trendle created the Lone Ranger for the radio, he gave his writers a code of behavior that the Lone Ranger and Tonto must live by. Jay and I were heroes to millions of kids, and to avoid disappointing them, we lived by Trendle's original rules:

- The Lone Ranger never smokes, never uses profanity, and never uses intoxicating beverages.
- The Lone Ranger is a man who can fight great odds, yet takes time to treat a bird with a broken wing.
- The Lone Ranger believes that our sacred American heritage provides that every individual has the right to worship God as he desires.
- Play down gambling and drinking scenes as far as possible, and keep the Lone Ranger out of saloons. When this cannot be avoided, try to make the saloon a cafe—and deal with waiters and food instead of bartenders and liquor.
- The Lone Ranger at all times uses precise speech, without slang or dialect. His grammar must be pure. He must make proper use of "who" and "whom," "shall," and "will," "I," and "me," etc.
- The Lone Ranger never shoots to kill. When he has to use guns, he aims to maim as painlessly as possible.

In addition, we were careful to be respectful to all people at all times. We never smoked when in costume. We showed respect for the police and the concepts of law and order. We always remembered that fair play and honesty were the most important qualities to get across to the kids.

For me, there was one more special rule: never appear in public without the mask.

By sticking with this code, and by making sure that *The Lone Ranger* episodes stuck with it, too, we gained not only the respect of our audience, but love, admiration, and trust. We earned that respect because we respected our audiences—especially the children. That's a lesson a lot of performers these days would do well to learn.

Those rules might seem a little out of date in the 1990s. But if they are, it's our loss. Because, even today, I often meet adults in their thirties, forties, or fifties who, as soon as they recognize me, suddenly become six years old again. You can see it in their eyes and hear it in their voices. They remember the character and what he stood for.

To them, the Lone Ranger is more than a childhood hero. He's a reminder of a time when they were still optimistic, when they still believed in happy endings, knew that good would always win out. Maybe to those "grown-up kids" the Lone Ranger is an ideal that means optimism is still possible, just like other "outdated" ideas like integrity, generosity, bravery, and kindness. And maybe, because they still cherish these ideas, they're a little more likely to pass them on to their own kids.

Lone Ranger Rock is now surrounded by a harsher, less heroic modern world, but it hasn't backed up an inch. The qualities that made the Lone Ranger great—and that the kids of several generations learned from him—haven't diminished, either. Maybe those qualities are harder to recognize, surrounded as they are by a world that pretends not to have time for them. But they live on, just like the character I have been so proud to portray. Those qualities will continue to live, long after I am gone.

As you can see, the Lone Ranger is more than just a role to me. Portraying the Lone Ranger on television and the movies and in personal appearances has been a source of great personal pride. It isn't too much to say that it literally changed my life.

But when I went in for my first interview, nearly fifty years ago, I wasn't looking for a life-changing experience— just a job. And the road that took me to that point was a long and winding one.

Guns blazing. Dust flying. Horses racing. The excitement was so overwhelming I could almost taste it. I gripped the cap pistol in my hand, my eyes glued to the action on the screen. I had spent an extra nickel for a chocolate bar, but I couldn't think about eating it now. There was too much going on. The action was incredible, and I was no less a part of it just because I was only in the audience and not riding with that glorious black-and-white posse. Physically, I was in the Devon Theater at Broadway and Granville in Chicago. But in my mind I was out West, astride a fast horse, upholding justice, fighting the bad guys. All of my friends enjoyed Western movies, too, but not like I did. To me, it was personal. I didn't know why. I just knew that I would give anything to be up there on the screen with Ken Maynard, Tom Mix, George O'Brien, William S. Hart, Harry Carey Sr.—so many wonderful cowboy heroes. On Saturdays I would pay my nickel, find my theater seat, and stay almost all day long, sitting through show after show of Westerns and serials, the most exciting movies a boy could hope to see. Later my pals and I would get together and reenact the films we had just seen, playing cowboys and Indians. I was *always* the hero.

It may sound strange, but that's what I wanted to be

when I grew up: a hero. Those great Western stars were more to me than just good guys in a movie who rode beautiful horses and brought justice to the men in the black hats. They stood for something. I guess for lack of a better phrase I'd call it the American spirit. They were brave and fast on the draw, to be sure, but they also embodied ideas like justice and fair play and patriotism. That struck a deep chord in me. My dream was that someday I could be like them. Not all dreams can come true in this life—but that one did. Little did I know while I sat there in the dark of the movie theater that one day *I* would be on the screen, and millions of kids would be sitting there in my place, cheering me on, dreaming dreams of heroism and adventure through the exploits of the Lone Ranger.

I suppose I was destined to be a patriotic American from the day I was born in Saint Luke's Hospital on the South Side of Chicago. My birthday, September 14, 1914, was the 100th anniversary of the writing of "The Star Spangled Banner." It isn't exactly like George M. Cohan being "born on the Fourth of July" but it's close enough for me.

I was named Jack Carlton Moore though someone made a mistake on the birth certificate and wrote "Carlson." I had a cousin (my father's sister's son) named Carlton whom I was named after. I went by Jack Carlton Moore (notice that it's "Jack" not "John") for years until I got to Hollywood and a producer named Eddie Small changed my name to Clayton. He said Clayton sounded like a good Southern name. Now, why he wanted me to have a good Southern name I couldn't tell you.

Sound confusing? It isn't, really. People who knew me as a child and as a young man always called me Jack. Most of my friends in Hollywood called me Clay.

On one side were the maids quarters and on the other a kind of utility room for outboard motors, guns, and fishing tackle. Right in the center was a bathroom. As far as I can recall, my family never used that third floor as a ballroom, although it certainly would have been something my mother would have enjoyed.

What my father enjoyed was hunting and fishing. The president of the South Bend Bait Company, Ira Henning, was a boyhood pal of my father's. Whenever some new kind of fishing or hunting equipment came in, Mr. Henning would send it to my father to experiment with and try out; that's how my father ended up with so much fishing tackle and so many guns. In the back of the family Cadillac, my father kept a small single-cylinder Johnson motor and a rowboat that folded up.

Dad would call us from the office and say, "Jackie, Howard, we are going fishing at Lake Zurich. Get ready!" The spur of the moment, just like that. We would put on our fishing equipment and take off. Often, instead of Lake Zurich, we might go to any of the small lakes outside of Chicago, in towns like Des Plaines, Illinois. Sometimes we went fishing for a week or two in Three Rivers, Wisconsin, or Fond Du Lac for the muskies and sturgeon. On those occasions we would take Frieda Wasserman, our German maid, with us, and my father would hire a guide. These were not little informal camping trips but real expeditions. My father always had two tents, one for the car and the equipment and another for sleeping. Frieda would have her kitchen tent with canvas shelves and the dishes and everything she needed. And we had portable toilets.

My father was quite a sportsman. He gave me my first gun and taught me to shoot. My brothers and I had our own trap guns and a clay pigeon arm to swing the clay pigeons out. My brothers and I would get behind this large thick board and fire when the target sailed through the air.

It's a little ironic to me that, although I've been shooting since I was a kid and I became famous as a great Western character who was a sure shot, in reality, I'm only a mediocre shot. That isn't to say that I'm no good with a gun. A stunt man named Tom Steele taught me all about handling a firearm with real panache—fancy draws, twirls, fast draws, and over the shoulder shots. I learned from Tom how to transfer from one hand to the other. In the real Old West, you would have been killed immediately if you did all that fancy stuff, but it was great fun to do and the fans of the Lone Ranger loved it.

We loved doing things together as a family, but my mother was rarely too enthusiastic about hunting and fishing. While we were up in the woods roughing it, she might go visit family members in California or go to Scottsdale, Arizona. She would take the train all by herself. Sometimes she would just stay home when we went fishing.

During one vacation in Wisconsin, we were planning to visit a nearby Indian reservation to attend a powwow. I was so excited at the prospect of seeing *real* Indians! The people who ran the lodge owned a dog that was used for bear hunting. He had recently been injured by a bear and wasn't feeling too well. I felt sorry for the poor dog, so while my father was shaving in the cabin, I went outside to pet the dog. As I bent toward him, I accidentally stepped on his foot. Without warning he snarled and bit me. His teeth went clear through my hand. My father heard my screams and came running outside, shaving lather all over his face. He quickly wrapped the wound with a bandage and then drove me to the nearest town to a doctor. There the wound was cauterized and bandaged properly.

"Let's get you home," my father said as we left the doctor's office.

I was stunned.

"You mean we can't go to the powwow?" I asked, heartbroken.

Dad said, "I didn't think you'd feel up to it." As if a little dog bite could keep me from meeting a true Indian chief! I assured him that I felt well enough to go; indeed, I wouldn't miss it for the world.

So we went, and it was just as wonderful as I had hoped it would be—a real big Indian show with ceremonial dances, singing and costumes, and other fascinating sights and sounds. I always knew that I wanted to grow up to be either a cowboy or a policeman, but this great powwow caused me to tip the scales toward the profession of cowboy. After all, how many Indian villages could I visit as a cop on the beat?

I can always remember my dad in a straw hat in the summertime. When I was fourteen or fifteen, in 1928, my father built a cabin at Loon Lake in Canada, which we always used as a summer home. We would go up every summer as soon as school was out and stay until the start of school in September. This was a beautiful, peaceful spot, and my mother enjoyed going there with us. Frieda would come, too, to work in the kitchen Dad built in the back of the main cabin. Guests would come up. Some stayed in the main cabin with us, but usually they slept in the boat house which had four bedrooms on the second floor. It was really a different time. My father would leave his business for the entire summer to stay with us at Loon Lake. With today's economy, something like that seems unbelievable, but that's the way things were.

We used to drive to Canada from Chicago maybe a week or so early as long as our grades were up. We would go from Chicago to Detroit where we went through customs. I remember a funny incident when we were trying to get through customs once. My father smoked Lucky Strike cigarettes in the flat tins; we called them "flat fifties." My father was a heavy cigarette smoker so he had maybe twenty-five tins of Lucky Strikes in the car. When we got to customs and opened up the suitcases, there were dozens of tins of cigarettes. This made the customs official very suspicious.

"Why are you transporting all of these cigarettes?" he asked. He obviously thought Dad was a cigarette smuggler.

My father nonchalantly pointed at Mother and us three kids. "Well," Dad said, "I smoke and my wife smokes, and we have to have enough cigarettes for the boys, too."

The customs man looked carefully at us—we were all just teenagers. "So," he said carefully, "These cigarettes are just for the family?"

"Absolutely," Dad said. We could tell the man was thinking it over. I guess he finally decided that providing us with cigarettes was bad, but not illegal. He let us pass over the border, and we laughed all the way into Canada. I still remember the rest of the Canadian journey we took so many times: through Windsor, Chatham, London, Paris, Bellville, Tweed, and finally to Loon Lake.

One of the greatest things about those summers on Loon Lake was the boating—and we had enough boats to go around. I had a speed boat called the Boyd Martin Bullet, and my brother had a sea sled with a racing Johnson motor. We also had a family boat and my father's fishing boat. The

Boyd Martin Bullet had a step in it with a ribbed canvas top, and I had a Johnson motor on the back of it, but it planed. My brother and I used to have boat races all the time. My father bought my mother a mahogany boat, with brass rivets, that held eight people. Speeding across the lake, feeling the wind and the spray of water in our faces, it was just like heaven. We never wanted those summers to end.

But they did end. It was great to get away on a camping trip or to our summer house in Loon Lake, but it was just as great to get back home. Chicago was a wonderful place to live, a terrific place to grow up. In those days it was already a big city, although not like it is now. There were plenty of wide open spaces, parks and woods, where we could play. From my earliest childhood, I had a passion for sports and athletics of all kinds. Sometimes they would flood the churchyard at Saint Gertrude's Catholic Church so we could ice skate. My father did that at home, too, flooding our yard to create a perfect little ice rink. We were big ice skaters in my family. My father had fancy skates and liked to do elaborate figure eights and other tricky moves. I think I started skating when I was three years of age. My first skates had double runners and clipped over my shoes. Later, my father let me use his fancy skates—I liked anything that had tricks to it. We also tobogganed on the gently sloping hills of Palos Park and went skiing in South Chicago. (I'll bet very few people go skiing in South Chicago these days!) If my father had business out in the suburbs, sometimes he would tie the toboggan to the back of the car and tow us through the snowy streets.

We loved having snowball fights—rough ones. We would soak the snowballs in water and make them ice balls. In those days the milk wagons were horse drawn.

One day while we were having a snowball fight, the horse-drawn milk wagon came by just as I threw a snowball at a friend of mine. He went back for it and ran right into the horse. It was so icy that the horse's feet flew into the air and he flipped over onto his side with a thud. Luckily he wasn't hurt, but we didn't stick around long enough to get in any trouble!

Charlie McCoy, a friend of my father's, had a farm out near Palos Park, and he started a bottled water company called Dienell Spring Water. McCoy's pet bear named Nell fell into the well one day and drowned. That's when Mr. McCoy named the water Dienell Spring Water—in memory of Nell.

Out at Mr. McCoy's farm, I had my first experience with owning a horse. My father gave my brothers and me a tiny horse, much smaller than a Shetland pony, which we kept out at the farm. It was really less like a horse than a collie dog. Not exactly a big, powerful steed like Silver, but it was a start. I was probably eight years old and dearly loved that little horse.

Living in Chicago had a great deal to do with the way my personal character developed. During your childhood, you form the values that will remain with you for life, and Chicago gave me a strong, Midwestern foundation of decency and morality. Of course, my values were also a result of my home life. My family was close and we spent a lot of time together having fun. In fact, although I was a Boy Scout—I went as far as second class in Boy Scouts—I never went on summer camping trips with the troop. I always went away with my family for the summer. That's the way I preferred it, too.

We lived on Glenwood Avenue in the Edgewater neighborhood. It was basically a Catholic neighborhood, although my family attended the Methodist/Presbyterian church. A lot of my friends went into the priesthood. Saint Ignatious Church was right on the corner down from my house.

In the neighborhood, I liked to hang around with my gang, the Glenwood Middies. If I ever knew what that name meant, I've forgotten. We wouldn't even have been able to spell it at the time. A "gang" in those days was nothing like what the word signifies today. We were just a group of kids who played together, had fun together. We often got into mischief, but never into trouble. A few streets over were the Wayne Avenue Middies, our rivals. We played baseball and football, had snowball fights in the wintertime and ice skated, played a little hockey with broomsticks, too. It was fun just being with the gang that lived in the neighborhood.

Of course, there were other kinds of gangs in Chicago in the 1920s. After the movies on Saturdays, I used to go down to my father's office in a one-story building at Twenty-Second and Michigan Avenue, across the street from the Lexington Hotel. One day when I was about seven years old, my father said, "Son, you want to see the big man?" He sat me down in a chair in front of the window and said, "Now, you keep staring across the street and you will see the big man come out."

I couldn't imagine what I was going to see, but I watched very, very closely. Suddenly five or six men stepped into the street, very briskly, with a no-nonsense air about them, as though they were checking the area out. Behind them came a small army of men, and in the center walked a man who didn't look very "big" at all. He was dressed in a blue suit, grey hat, grey spats, and a blue double-breasted topcoat.

It was Al Capone.

A Lincoln drove up. Another car pulled up next to it, and

another car pulled up in the rear. Capone entered the Lincoln, which immediately drove away. Moments later, his son Bobby Capone came out. His bodyguard looked as if he was six foot, eight inches—a big fella. In those days, we had a toy called a diablo: two sticks connected by a string with a peg in the center. Little Bobby Capone had a diablo—and so did that fierce-looking body guard. They were both playing with their toys as though they hadn't a care in the world. I don't know if my father actually knew Al Capone. I think that he rented a couple of stores to Capone's men, who would run them as florist shops or something. Whether or not they actually sold flowers, I don't know.

When he was still very young, my brother Sprague went to work with Dad. I can remember that office as if I saw it just this morning. My father's space was in the back, his desk and chair behind a partition. Next came my brother's desk. The secretary was situated up in the front. It was always kind of a special thing to visit my father. I had to look neat and tidy when I went to his office.

Sprague never graduated from high school, but he went to prep school at Notre Dame in South Bend, Indiana, for one year. I don't know why he didn't graduate from high school; Sprague was extremely smart, a very sharp guy.

When I was young, I went to Hayt Grammar School. What I remember most about Hayt was the wonderful playground there, with rings and bars for acrobatics, and swings and slides. Even after I no longer attended the school, I used to go back to work out on the rings. Of course, to a kid, the name of the school was too much of a temptation. When we had to write essays and themes, we were always instructed to write our names on one side of the paper and "Hayt School" on the other. I could never resist writing "I Hayt School." The teachers, for some reason, never found that to be as funny as I did.

I was an ambitious, hard-working, aggressive kid. I got an allowance of twenty-five cents a week, but that wasn't enough for me. In the wintertime in Chicago, when I was about nine or ten, a couple of boys would pitch in with me—I would kind of organize them—and we would shovel sidewalks and driveways. I charged fifty cents to do a driveway and paid the other two kids ten or fifteen cents because I owned the company. When it snowed, we would get up early in the morning, go around the neighborhood, and drum up business.

I used to stand outside the grocery store, and when I saw the women with packages in their arms, I would go up to them and offer to help carry the groceries home. When I wasn't carrying packages or shoveling sidewalks, I would go out to the different apartment buildings in the neighborhood and sell magazines like *The Saturday Evening Post* and *The Lady's Home Journal*. I did pretty well for myself.

My brother Howard was not nearly as industrious as I was. On Friday nights, he would say casually, "So, Jack, what are we going to do tomorrow?"

Of course, tomorrow was Saturday and there was only one place I would be on a Saturday!

"I am going to see William S. Hart at the picture show. *And*," I would continue, mentioning a very important part of the plan, "I am going to get myself some popcorn and candy."

Howard would lower his head a little and say, "Gee, I wish I could go...." He would give me that pathetic look and pull out his pockets to show me how empty they were. I knew it was an act, but I couldn't take it. Besides, I always had a little extra money from all of my odd jobs.

"Aw, all right," I would say, giving in. "I'll pay. You can go to the show with me."

I think that says a lot about our relationship. I thought the world of him, and even though he was older, Howard always looked up to me a little. It may have been because I was so active all the time and he was not as involved in athletics like I was. Whenever I had an hour off, I would go over to Hayt School, go into the gym or out to the playground, and work on the rings or the horizontal bar. Howard loved music. He could play any instrument—just pick an instrument up for the first time and play something. I was the athlete, Howard was the musician, and Sprague was only interested in girls.

I went to Sullivan Junior High School and Senn High School. It's funny how many little details I remember about Senn in particular. The athletic coach's name was Al Bergman. I remember always crossing the football field to school. And I have fond memories of those corridors—in fact, I think I could still walk right up the steps and find my locker, even today. Senn was a terrific school; everyone was very proud of being a student there. I belonged to a fraternity called Alpha Sigma Lambda. On Saturday nights we would go down to the Edgewater Beach Hotel and dance to Paul Whiteman and his orchestra. I suppose the Charleston was the dance of the moment—those were really great times.

I was a drum major at Sullivan and played the bugle. Although I loved athletics, I didn't participate in many team sports at either Sullivan or Hayt School when I was a kid. I much preferred spending time at the Illinois Athletic Club—which we called the IAC—swimming, tumbling, lifting weights, and jumping on the trampoline.

When I was nine years old, I had started going to the

IAC with my father and brothers. The IAC was a wonderful place. It had a gymnasium and swimming pool, hardball court, handball courts, and social functions. We went there about once a week and it was there that I became interested in swimming and gymnastics. The club was downtown, across the street from the Art Institute of Chicago. When I became older, I took the elevated trains (the El) to the club, but in those early days my father would drop me off or, better still, come in with my brothers and me to swim or work out.

I won the Illinois Athletic Club championship for swimming in the 100-yard dash when I was fifteen years old. I spent a lot of time down at the pool with a great coach, Bill Bachrach, and a training coach who was nicknamed WXYZ (I have no idea why). Bill Bachrach also trained a young swimmer at the club named Johnny Weissmuller. Johnny and I were on friendly terms. Neither of us could have dreamed that one day we would cross paths on publicity tours—me as the Lone Ranger and Johnny as Jungle Jim.

The first time I ever saw Johnny swim, I knew he had something special. They had a race from a spot on Lake Michigan near the Drake Hotel (where Johnny was a bell hop) out to the pumping station and back. Both Johnny and his brother Pete entered the race. Johnny won easily. It was really something to see. Coach Bill Bachrach thought so, too. He asked Johnny if he would like to be a world champion swimmer. Johnny said, "Who wouldn't?" I don't think Johnny took the idea very seriously. But Bill told Johnny to come to the Athletic Club to talk with him. And Bill did indeed coach Johnny Weissmuller into becoming a world champion swimmer.

⋈

One day at the Illinois Athletic Club, I was doing some

acrobatic work by myself and caught the eye of Johnny Behr, the athletic director of the IAC. He told me that he thought that I had the strength and coordination to work on the trapeze. It looked like fun, so I decided to try it out.

I took to it immediately. I loved the sensation of flying through the air, doing somersaults, twisters, and other tricks, swinging high above the ground. When I was young I only "flew" to be caught by a more experienced trapeze artist like Johnny. After I grew better at it, I was taught to catch.

All we had at the IAC was one trapeze. Dismounting from the trapeze, we landed on mats—we never had a net. With just a single trapeze, there could be no going from man to man; we would just swing off of a pedestal and do a somersault and land on the mats. Howard liked the trapeze, too. He never wanted to do it professionally, but enjoyed practicing up at the club. One day he did a trick—rather, he *almost* did it—fell down, hit his forehead, and sprained his neck. So that was the end of Howard doing trapeze.

Of course, we always trained wearing safety belts. The safety belts kept us from getting seriously injured, but there were always pains connected with trapeze work: blistered hands or sprained arms. Sometimes while catching a trick, you would get hit in the face and end up with a nosebleed. But every sport has its dangers. The thrill of trapeze work and the sheer fun of what we were doing far outweighed any occasional discomfort.

After working together at the IAC informally for a few years, Johnny Behr suggested that we form a real trapeze act. He even had a name all ready, the Flying Behrs. I was excited at the prospect of working up a spectacular act to perform in front of appreciative crowds, so I immediately agreed. We asked some other friends to join us, terrific trapeze artists,

Sven Matthews, Robert Troush, Henry Montoya, and Bob Vin.

The first performance of the Flying Behrs took place at the IAC's annual water show, for members only. Because the IAC had no net, we placed our trapeze above the pool; we would use the water to land on.

As we began performing professionally, we began to acquire the tools we needed, like real safety nets. And we built a large trapeze over at Johnny Behr's house. At the time, I don't know if I wanted to make trapeze work a career or not. Probably not, because my childhood goals really hadn't changed: I still wanted to be either a policeman or a cowboy.

I was so focused on the trapeze act that it didn't leave a great deal of time for social activities at school. After class, I would go down to the IAC to work out or go home to practice on my own equipment. This schedule didn't leave me any time to play on the high school football or basketball teams, and I'm sure I missed a great many extracurricular activities. However, I never regretted it. I was in tip-top shape and working with excellent athletes. It was a very exciting, rewarding time in my life.

Most of the Flying Behrs' performances took place around the Chicago area, although we did occasionally travel as far as Detroit or Erie, Pennsylvania. Our first paying job brought the entire group $1200, out of which came our expenses. Johnny Behr acted as our booking agent as well as our coach. I recall that we played in an old theater—a vaudeville house, I think—on the West Side of Chicago. We hung our trapeze rigging from the catwalk above the stage.

But our biggest break came when we were booked at the 1934 Chicago World's Fair.

We performed there for the greater part of that summer. I would travel to the fairground on the El to do two shows a day, an afternoon and an evening show. The announcer was Norman Ross Sr. There was also a water show after our performance: divers and slapstick on the diving board with performers like Boyd Little and Larry Lawdell, very clever comedians of the diving board. The wife of Richard Farnsworth, later a very fine stuntman and actor, was on the show as part of a girl's swimming act. Dick introduced me to her years later and she said, "I know Clayton. I was at the World's Fair with him in 1934."

Our act was not all that different from those of other trapeze artists. We had two catchers, one on the left and one on a pedestal in the center. I was almost always a catcher, but I could do a pretty good one-and-a-half or double somersault myself. One trick we did that seemed to particularly thrill audiences was the "passing leap." In this tricky maneuver, one acrobat would leave the trapeze, flying toward the catcher on the left. At the same time, the man on the pedestal would take the trapeze and swing out over the top—the two men would pass in midair!

Of course, we acted like daredevils—and trapeze work *is* dangerous—but we weren't foolhardy. Some trapeze acts take pride in working without a net, but we were smarter than that! We always used a net, unless we were performing over a swimming pool.

One of the prime attractions at the World's Fair was Sally Rand, a very well-known dancer of the day. The reason that she was so well-known was that she danced wearing fans or balloons, and *nothing* but fans or balloons. It was, by today's standards, a very modest act; the audience never actually *saw* anything. Miss Rand would move a fan away and then put another in its place before you knew it—she was quite an artist with those fans. Still, being young men, the Flying

Behrs caught quite a few of Sally Rand's performances. We found her quite fascinating.

The Flying Behrs performed so much during that summer of 1934 that we decided to try something different once the World's Fair was over. We started working on the trampoline instead of the trapeze. We had actually been doing certain trampoline stunts during our regular show, but now we decided to concentrate just on the trampoline. It turned out to be an unlucky change.

CHAPTER TWO

A Cowboy Actor in the Big Apple

When I was a small child, whenever anyone asked me what I wanted to be when I grew up, I would always answer one of two ways. According to my mood at the time, I said either, "I want to be a policeman" or "I want to be a cowboy." Sometimes I wanted to grow into some combination of the two—I guess you could say that becoming the Lone Ranger was the perfect way to be a policeman *and* a cowboy.

My ambitions never changed much, no matter what else I was doing. Even when I was performing with the Flying Behrs, I never thought that I would become a professional trapeze artist. I loved doing it, it was fun and exciting, but trapeze work was always a sideline, a hobby.

Only one time in my youth did I consider another career: I decided that I wanted to become a doctor. My father approved of this ambition—he probably thought it was a little more respectable than cowboy—and arranged for me to go live with my great-aunt in Daytona Beach, Florida. I needed physics and chemistry to get my graduation diploma from high school, and Daytona Beach High School had an excellent science department. I think that my father believed that I would study harder and concentrate on my studies if I lived in a new environment. He had lived with my great-aunt when he was younger and thought that it was the perfect place for me.

He was right. I liked being in Florida, which was quite a change from winter in Chicago. And I enjoyed getting to know my great-aunt. For about six months I was happy and hard working. But my desire to become a doctor turned out to be a whim. The more I thought about it, the less I could see myself in that profession for the rest of my life. Physicians do such important work, and I admired them so much that I thought it would be a wonderful, rewarding way to live. But in my heart of hearts, I knew it wasn't for me. I tried my best, but it didn't take me long to realize that I wasn't cut out for medicine.

One day early in the spring I got a call from Johnny Behr. "Hey Jack," he said, "The Flying Behrs are going on the road again."

"When?" I asked.

"Right away, this summer," he said. "We need a flier. How about it?"

That really sounded like fun. I missed performing. There was a wonderful gymnasium at Daytona Beach High School, and I still spent a great deal of my free time working out, keeping fit. But I couldn't do much trapeze work there.

"Sorry, Johnny," I said sadly. "I can't. It's only a few weeks until graduation."

Johnny was disappointed, but he understood that my education was more important. If I was going to become a doctor, I would have to concentrate on my studies and leave everything else behind. The trouble was, I didn't want to be a doctor anymore. I knew it wasn't for me. Right or wrong, I was going to have to follow my own heart. After thinking it over for several days, and talking with my parents about my decision, I called Johnny Behr.

"Johnny," I said, "you've got yourself a trapeze performer."

I left Daytona Beach a few days later and never graduated from high school.

But even though I couldn't resist going on the road with the Flying Behrs, I knew that my future did not lie in that direction. I loved the athletic challenge of what we were doing, but even more, I loved performing in front of appreciative audiences. Little by little, I began to realize that show business was my future—not trapeze work, but acting. The little boy who dreamed of becoming a movie cowboy was learning that such a wonderful thing might actually be possible. Now when I went to the movies, it was with the pleasant—though slightly scary—realization that I could do that. I could really *do* that!

Besides, something happened about then that completely erased the possibility of a continued career on the trapeze. After the World's Fair when the Flying Behrs added trampoline stunts to their show, I landed wrong during a workout and bounced off the side of the trampoline, injuring my knee. I thought it was only a bad sprain at first, but when it didn't get any better, I learned that it would require surgery. I knew that I had to start thinking about a new career—and this injury clinched it.

But if I was going to be an actor, I had no idea how or where to start. I didn't know anybody else who had become a movie cowboy, so there was no one I could turn to for advice. I did, however, have one idea about how to take the first tiny step. My older brother Sprague had been modeling for some time for several local newspapers and catalogs. He and several other people began to suggest that I might consider a career as a model, too. I thought it over and gradually it began to seem like a really good idea. People had often been nice enough to tell me I had a handsome face. And through my years of athletic training, I was in superb physical condition. I knew that I didn't want to make modeling my livelihood, but I realized that it would give me some valuable experience in how to behave in front of the camera. Besides, the money wasn't bad, either. Sprague only pursued modeling as a sideline before committing to full-time work with my father at the real estate office. But I was ambitious, with a pretty good head for business. I was determined to make good at whatever I tried.

In no time, after listening to my brother's advice, I was modeling in Chicago with the Al and Connie Seaman Agency. I did newspaper and catalog advertisements—including several for Sears Roebuck—and specialized in clothing ads. But although Chicago was a wonderful city, I knew that it didn't offer the theatrical opportunities I would need to get started in my new profession. Since I had ambitions to get into the movies, I considered packing up and moving to Hollywood. But I thought I had better learn to act first. For that, there was only one place to go—New York.

One of my friends in Chicago was a very nice fellow who called himself by a stage name, Alan Curtis (his real name was Harold Neberroth). He also had aspirations to be an actor but worked as a model and had done a few commercial photo shoots with me. Alan encouraged me to go to New York. He said, "You can always find work modeling, but if you're in New York, you can get some stage experience, too." I told him that what I *really* wanted to be was a cowboy actor. "It doesn't matter," Alan said. "You need acting experience, and New York is the place to get it." Alan, by the way, was later a contract player at RKO and other studios, and appeared in many, many films.

I talked it over with my parents. They agreed that I had to make the move if I was ever going to succeed in show business. They were sad to see me go, and I was very sad to leave them behind. But it was powerfully exciting, too—the start of a whole new life.

In 1935 I boarded a train bound for New York. I carried with me a letter of reference from the Seaman Agency. They had advised me to make an appointment with John Robert Powers, head of one of the most important modeling agencies in New York. I still wasn't sure how this move was going to help me become a cowboy actor, but it seemed logical that the best way to become an actor was to be where other actors were. Once I was there and started to learn the ropes, I could more clearly map out a plan of action. In the meantime, modeling would continue to support me.

Mr. Powers received me very warmly; my letter of reference from Al and Connie Seaman must have made an impression on him. I showed him my portfolio, which included several ad campaigns from Chicago.

"You're a natural for this line of work," Mr. Powers said. "I think you're capable of doing much more than just clothing ads."

"What do you mean?" I asked.

"You have a very dramatic quality," he said. "You don't just pose—you *act* the part. We could use you for book covers, or for the illustrations in mystery magazines."

This was very exciting to me. I felt that I was actually getting some acting experience at the same time that I was doing a job with which I already felt comfortable.

John Robert Powers was a very friendly fellow, a dapper, nice-looking dark-haired guy. He introduced me to one of his top models, Harry Connover, and asked Harry to take me to the different commercial photography studios around town, to drop off photographs and make sure that they knew about me. Unfortunately, just as I arrived in New York, there was an elevator strike—and it seemed as if every one of these photography studios was on the top floor of ten or twelve story buildings. Building after building after building. It was a good thing I was in such top condition because we really got a workout visiting these places. Every day for a week, we went from studio to studio, leaving photographs with various commercial photographers, hoping that they would remember me when they needed a model of my type.

New York turned out to be a lucky place for me—at first. I began working almost immediately, not only in clothing and automobile ads such as you would see in the Sears Roebuck catalogs, but as Mr. Powers had suggested, in more dramatic kinds of photographs and illustrations for love and romance stories, true stories, crime stories—every kind of newspaper and magazine story imaginable. One day I was decked out in a top hat and tails, doing a classy perfume ad with Gay Hayden; the next day I was a swarthy thug on the cover of a crime magazine. I even appeared as the "after" in a "before and after" muscle-building advertisement.

At about this time, I met Tom Neal, a struggling actor. Because he wasn't getting many parts in stage productions, he would occasionally come up to the Powers Agency and try to get jobs as a model. Tom was a very handsome, charismatic guy, and I knew he was going to be successful in show business. We had a lot in common and became very close friends. We decided that we should share an apartment to save money. We found an inexpensive place at the Montclair Hotel (later the Belmont Plaza) on Forty-Ninth Street and Lexington.

There were many times, of course, when we both really *needed* to save money. Even though Mr. Powers got me steady work sometimes, there were the inevitable periods when, as the saying goes, I couldn't get arrested. Like all aspiring artists, I put in plenty of time suffering and paying my dues. I remember that around Easter that year things were pretty bad financially. I had never asked my dad for any money, no matter how bad things got, and I wouldn't even *consider* asking Mr. Powers for an advance, although I'm certain he would have given me one. It might sound stubborn on my part, but I was always the kind of person who wanted to be responsible. I never wanted anybody's charity. Of course, that kind of attitude isn't always easy. Now I was really broke, and my pride wasn't going to pay the rent.

It was a miserable time. I really missed my family, so as Easter approached, I sent my mother a holiday telegram, then went to get something to eat. There were only two places where I could afford to eat—a little diner called the Blue Bowl and a Greek automat. At the automat, for a nickel and a dime, you could get sandwiches and vegetables, and for a quarter you could get a whole meal. At the end of the day, I had thirty-five cents in my pocket. My rent had to be paid at the Montclair Hotel but I had no way of coming up with the money.

The next morning I didn't even feel like getting out of bed. It was one of the lowest times in my life. Suddenly the phone rang. It was someone from the Powers Agency.

"Mr. Moore," she said, "you aren't booked for a photo shoot today, are you?"

I thought to myself, "Are you kidding?" but I just said, "No, I'm free today."

She sounded relieved. "Good. We need you to model some tennis clothes for a magazine ad." While she gave me the address where I was to report, I felt like leaping in the air. The job paid twenty-five dollars *cash*, which I received at the end of the day. I could pay the rent, have a good meal, and still have money left over! This experience made me think about how quickly life can turn around, from bad to good, from down to up. I was to learn that lesson a few more times over the course of my life.

Things went better financially from that time on, but I was beginning to feel frustrated in New York. I was really no closer to becoming an actor than when I had lived in Chicago. My friend Tom Neal was constantly auditioning for stage roles. Sometimes he got the parts—more often, he didn't. I didn't want to live like that. It wasn't the kind of acting I was interested in. I realized that by coming to New York, I had only been postponing the inevitable.

What was my dream? To become a cowboy actor.

Where do cowboy actors work?

Hollywood.

CHAPTER THREE

Hollywood!

I left for Los Angeles in 1937. Although I was determined to be a Western actor and get into the movies, I had only one very slight connection to the motion picture business. When my mother was a girl, she knew a man who worked at Columbia Pictures out in California. When I left Chicago, she said, "When you get to Los Angeles, look up this friend of mine." Today, I'm sorry to say, I don't remember his name or in what capacity he worked at Columbia. But as soon as I arrived on the West Coast, I called him from my cousin's house, told him who I was, and said that I would like to meet him and talk to him. He invited me to the studio.

I suppose he was just being polite because of his acquaintance with my mother, because when I got to the studio, I was sent up to his office, but talked to him for only about a minute and a half before he gave me the brush off. "Why don't you go down and see Joe Rifkin, our talent scout?" he said.

I said, "All right, nice meeting you, thank you," and went down to Joe Rifkin's office. Mr. Rifkin asked me what kind of experience I'd had. I said, rather importantly, "Well, I've been in New York."

He said, "I like your look, kid. Were you doing stage work in New York?"

Of course, I hadn't done any acting at all, but I said, "Sure."

"I'll tell you what," Mr. Rifkin continued, "I will do something for you." He picked up the telephone. Now Irene Dunne had just finished shooting a picture, and the crew was still on the set down on a soundstage. Mr. Rifkin got the director on the phone and said, "I would like to shoot a test, just a few feet, of a young man who is here in my office." The director agreed.

Irene Dunne's cameraman was still there, and he took a silent test of me. All I had to do was walk in, walk down some steps, step right up to the camera, and smile. It was easy—just like the modeling I had done in Chicago and New York. It only took about half an hour. When it was over, I went back into Joe Rifkin's office.

He said, "The cameraman liked you very much—he liked your looks. Let me give you a script and you can read up on it and then, a week from now, come here and we can get a girl to read the script with you."

That seemed simple enough, so I said, "All right," and took the script, went home and memorized it. In the meantime Mr. Rifkin set up a meeting in his office with a director and an associate producer. When I returned a week later, they were there along with a beautiful young actress they had brought in to read the script with me. Her name was Jacqueline Wells.

The scene, from Frank Capra's *It Happened One Night*, which had been released three years earlier, had originally been performed by Clark Gable and Claudette Colbert. I knew the part pretty well, so the actress and I started reading. I got about a paragraph into it when the two men walked out of the room. Then Jacqueline Wells followed them.

Joe Rifkin stared at me with a stricken look on his face. He didn't speak for a very long time. Finally, very deliberately, he said, "I thought you said you were on Broadway."

I said, "No, but I *tried* to get on Broadway."

Mr. Rifkin said, "Kid, you better go to dramatic school." He got on the phone and called Doc Fleishman, a well-known dramatic coach. He told Doc that he had a young fellow in his office who had bluffed his way into Columbia Studios. "He's a great looking kid," Mr. Rifkin said, "but he's a lousy actor. He needs to learn how to read a line."

I didn't take what he said personally—I knew he was right. However, I was very anxious to learn, to better myself. Doc Fleishman accepted me, and I studied dramatics there for six months. I didn't have the money to pay for it, so my father sent me twenty-five dollars a week to help with my acting lessons. That was a lot of money in those days, but I knew it was worth it. A lot of people in the picture business studied with Doc Fleishman. His roster of students was very impressive.

It was a humbling way to start out, but the experience did me a world of good and had a great effect on my life for years to come. For one thing, Joe Rifkin later became my agent, after he left Columbia Studios. And at Doc Fleishman's, in 1938, I met Rand Brooks, who would become one of my closest, lifelong friends.

After six months of study, Joe Rifkin set up another screen test. This time I was scared to death. I knew I could bluff my way through once, but not twice. This time I had to deliver the goods. I remember that Rudy Wilcox was the director of this test, and Les White was the cameraman.

Luckily, the test went fine. I was still a beginner as an actor, but I proved to them—and myself—that I had what it takes to work in movies.

At about that same time, Brian Foy, a producer at Warner Bros., was looking for a tall, dark-haired, well-built man to put into an action film. He knew Doc Fleishman because he regularly sent actors to study with him. When Foy described the type he was looking for, Doc immediately thought of me and suggested my name to him.

I was ecstatic—and a little nervous—when I heard the news. I immediately made an appointment to see Brian Foy. When I arrived at his office, he wasn't there. But there was a little girl sitting there. She was about five or six years old, very cute and talkative. She loved horses and was thrilled when I told her that I often rode. I got on my hands and knees and said, "Get on." So she climbed on my back and started pretending that she was riding a horse. I galloped around the office, whinnying and neighing, and she was giggling and shouting "Giddap!"

Just then Brian Foy walked into the office. He just looked at me, down on the floor, giving this little girl a horsey ride. I got up as quickly as I could, trying to maintain as much dignity as possible under the circumstances. I said, "Mr. Foy, Doc Fleishman sent me to see you."

"Oh yeah," Mr. Foy said, "you must be Jack Moore." He looked me over for a moment. "Mr. Moore," he said, "I'm going to put you under a stock contract with the studio."

I was stunned. I hadn't taken a test or anything and here I was under contract at Warner Bros. I didn't know exactly what to say. Mr. Foy smiled and called the little girl over to him. "I see you've already met my daughter," he said. The little girl was grinning ear to ear. "He's a good horsey," she said. I laughed along with Mr. Foy, but inside I was thinking, "I just hope I'm good enough!"

I was at Warner Bros. for six months. I never did any real parts, only bits and one liners. The first film I appeared in was *When Were You Born?* (1938) with Anna May Wong; then *The Cowboy from Brooklyn* (1938) with Dick Powell, Pat O'Brien, and Priscilla Lane; and *Crime School* (1938) with the Dead End Kids and Humphrey Bogart. I only made seventy-five dollars a week, but after making nothing for so long, that seemed pretty good to me. Besides, it was a great learning experience—I never forgot that I was there because I gave a little girl a horsey ride.

In addition to small parts in film, all the contract players at the studio continued to study dramatics. The studio system of those days was really great for teaching you your craft as a performer. Often we would produce entire plays, just for the experience—no audience would ever see them. I acted in a workshop play called *The Shining Hour*, and my co-stars included Susan Hayward, Carole Landis, Jeffrey Lynn, all kids who were starting in the business just like I was.

Even though I was only a bit player in the Warner Bros. stock company, I took my job seriously. In 1938 a terrible flood hit the area. In my little '28 Ford, I fought my way to the studio gate at Barham and Pass Avenue. I was the only one who got to the studio that day.

Soon, however, I would have another studio to be serious about. Billy Grady, a casting director at MGM, was looking for a young, athletic fellow. He described the kind of actor he needed to Brian Foy. Mr. Foy said, "We have somebody right here that fits that description perfectly—Jack Moore."

By that time, Joe Rifkin was my agent, so they called him. It was common in those days for one studio to borrow an actor from another. Joe called me and said that Billy Grady at MGM wanted to see me. However, to see him, I had to have an agent by the name of Frank Orsati. Billy Grady would not see any actors unless they were with the Orsati Brothers, who were *the* agents in the business. They handled nearly everyone at MGM.

So I had a problem. Joe Rifkin was not only my agent. He was a friend and had been very helpful to me. But being an ambitious man wanting to get ahead, I knew what I had to do. I called Joe Rifkin on the phone, made an appointment, and went to his office. Rifkin was a prince of a man. He said, "I can have you released from your contract with me whenever you want."

"I would like it now," I said.

Frank Orsati took me over to Metro and introduced me to Billy Grady. He liked my looks and said that he wanted to set up a screen test. In the meantime I called Tom Neal in New York and asked how he was doing. Tom had just finished a play with Maria Ouspenskaya called *Daughters of Atrias*. Tom asked how I was doing and I said, "Great! I've been under contract at Warner Bros. and now I'm going to be at Metro." Tom was very impressed. I said, "Come on out. Pickins are easy!" He got on the next train and came out to California. I picked him up at Union Station and took him back to my cousin Warren's house; he stayed with us there.

How Tom got over to Metro, I do not know, but he met Billy Grady, who said he wanted to do a test of Tom. Mr. Grady said, "Will you do the test with Jack Carlton?" Grady had no idea that we not only knew each other but were living in the same place. So Tom and I made the test together, and they signed both of us to stock contracts at Metro. Just as at Warner Bros., I would be making seventy-five dollars a week. We studied acting with Lillian Burns, the wife of the great MGM director George Sidney, who made so many wonderful musicals like *The Harvey Girls* (1946) and *Show Boat* (1951).

My career at Metro was on pretty much the same track as at Warner Bros. For instance, I had a single line in *Sergeant Madden* (1939) with Wallace Beery and Laraine Day. Also as at Warners, I stayed at Metro for six months. I didn't make much headway there, and they were going to drop me from my contract. But, once again, luck was with me.

A producer named Eddie Small, head of Edward Small Productions, had dinner with Billy Grady at about this time. Eddie Small said, "Look, we had Jon Hall signed up for a picture, but Sam Goldwyn won't let him loose to do it. We're looking for a six-foot-one, six-foot-two, dark-haired fellow to put in *South of Pago Pago*."

"I've got just the guy," Billy Grady said. He called me in to his office. It was the classic good news/bad news situation. "Jack," he said, "we are dropping you from your stock contract." I guess I had seen it coming, but it was still an unpleasant shock. I started to speak, and Mr. Grady held up his hand. "*But!*" he said, "Edward Small is looking for a young fella to put in *South of Pago Pago* and your name has been mentioned to him. He wants to see you." Al Orsati took me over to meet Eddie Small.

When I walked out of Small's office an hour later, I was signed to an exclusive contract with Edward Small Productions for the princely sum of $250 a week. At last, I thought, I have reached the big time.

Besides the money, Edward Small would make another

big change in my life. He didn't think my name, Jack Carlton, had enough personality. He asked me what I thought about changing it to Clayton Moore, which he thought had a nice ring to it. It didn't take me long to decide. *I* thought Clayton Moore had a nice ring to it, too. And I've been Clayton Moore ever since.

I began to rehearse for my leading role. *South of Pago Pago* (1940) was set in the South Seas, and I had to learn to perform a kind of native dance. I worked with a beautiful young actress named Olympe Bradna, who was, after Frances Farmer, the second female lead in the film. Hollywood was then, as it is now, a hotbed of gossip. Pretty soon the gossip columns began running items like this one written by Ed Sullivan: "Ethel Butterworth and Douglas Montgomery are churning up an old feeling. Judy Canova and Bob Lowry an item, ditto Olympe Bradna and Clayton Moore." The truth is that Olympe and I were never an "item." In fact, because of my love of horses, I remember being most interested in learning about her uncle Fred Bradna, the equestrian director of the Ringling Brothers and Barnum and Bailey Show.

Of course, the truth never has much to do with what people in Hollywood believe, as I found out when I struck up a very close friendship with one of movies' most glamorous stars, Lupe Velez.

Tom Neal and I used to go with some of our bachelor actor pals, like Dennis O'Keefe and John Carroll, to all the great night spots. One night we were at La Conga, having a grand old time, when a friend, Art LaShelle, came over to the table and said, "Clay, do you know Lupe Velez?"

Of course, I knew *about* her, but I had never met her. She had been linked with several Hollywood stars, including a very long, intense relationship with Johnny Weissmuller. They finally married, but it was a stormy union, and they divorced in 1933.

"No, I don't know her," I said. "Do you?"

"Yeah," Art said. "She wants to meet you."

Well, that was very flattering. I told Art that I was willing to meet her whenever she liked.

Art said, "She is giving a party Sunday at her home, and she would like you to come." I told him I would be there. The other guys at the table were very impressed.

That Sunday, I arrived at Lupe's beautiful house on Rodeo Drive. Art was there to meet me and to introduce me to Lupe. It was a very enjoyable afternoon. When the party was breaking up, she asked me to stay for dinner, and I replied that I would love to stay.

Even though it was just dinner for two, I didn't get the idea that Lupe had romance on her mind, and I was right. Something was bothering her. She told me that she was having trouble getting work in Hollywood. It had gotten so bad that she had gone to England to make a couple of films there.

"Now that I am back in town," she said, "I need to get some positive publicity."

"I understand," I said. "But what does that have to do with me?"

"You're a very handsome man," she said. "I have to be seen in all the right places, but I cannot go there unescorted. I would like you to take me to Ciro's, the Macombo, the Trocadero, or the Coconut Grove."

"I'm sorry Miss Velez," I said. "I don't think I can help you, although I'd love to. I'm just a contract player. I can't go to places like that. I can't afford it."

"Don't worry about that," she said. "These won't be dates. They're strictly business. I'll take care of everything."

All she wanted was to have publicity photos taken in all of these glamorous restaurants and nightclubs, to let Hollywood know that she was back in town. I had to think it over for a minute. Hmm, going out to expensive spots night after night with a gorgeous movie star—it certainly did seem like a rough way to spend my time.

Although we approached this as a business arrangement—all smoke and no fire—I genuinely came to like Lupe. We became very good friends. Lupe was a lovely lady. Her nickname was the Mexican Spitfire, and she *was* a spitfire when she was out in public. But in her home, she was genteel and intelligent. We used to go to the fights on Friday night at the Olympic Auditorium. Lupe would never arrive during the first round, but would come in about the second round. She liked to make an impressive entrance, driving up in front of the auditorium in her Dusenburg automobile. She was always beautifully dressed. When we went to the fights, she would take her rings off—she had a lot of rubies and diamonds—and she would put them in my coat pocket and push the handkerchief over them. I'll never forget the sight of Lupe, covered in expensive furs, sitting there yelling at the top of her lungs, "Kill the bum! Kill him!"

Of course, her publicity plan worked like a charm. In no time our pictures were appearing in newspapers and movie magazines, and the columnists were beginning to mention us. Once, when I was working on *Kit Carson* and wore my hair long for the part, Louella Parsons wrote that I was trying to look like Johnny Weissmuller. Knowing Johnny as I did, I took it as a compliment. I don't think I ever mentioned Lupe's name to Johnny.

Another time Louella Parsons wrote, "It looks like wedding bells for Lupe Velez and Clayton Moore." Lupe called Louella Parsons on the phone and read the riot act to her. I remember how infuriated she was, and you didn't want to get on Lupe's bad side.

Lupe drank "French seventy-fives," champagne with brandy; that was her favorite drink. Anyone who came to her table had an open bar. Lupe *always* picked up the tab. I remember watching her tip people ten and fifteen dollars for parking her Dusenburg. I don't know where her money came from, but there always seemed to be plenty of it.

She was, of course, a vivacious personality, but sometimes I saw another, sadder, side of her. Once she pointed to a picture of Gary Cooper and said quietly, "There is the only man I ever loved." I admired her very much and hoped that someday she would meet someone who would make her truly happy. Unfortunately, that never happened. Lupe killed herself in 1944.

>o<

Oddly enough, after having signed me for the express purpose of replacing Jon Hall in *South of Pago Pago*, Eddie Small informed me that he was able to borrow Hall from Goldwyn after all. I wasn't going to star in *South of Pago Pago*. In fact, I wasn't going to be in the picture at all. However, I wasn't discouraged because I had the feeling that Eddie Small was really behind me and was going to give me bigger and better roles in upcoming pictures.

That turned out to be the case. I was given a supporting role in his production of *Kit Carson* (1940), directed by George B. Seitz Sr. (Incidentally, George Seitz Jr. directed many of the early *Lone Ranger* episodes.) Jon Hall was once again the star in *Kit Carson* and the excellent cast included Ward Bond, Dana Andrews, and the beautiful Lynn Bari. I played Paul Terry, the leader of a wagon train, who asks Kit Carson to guide the group along the Oregon Trail into California. The location scenes were filmed in Tuba City, Arizona, a spectacular location. My parents and brother Howard came out to visit during the filming. For an independent production, *Kit Carson* was given great production values and was filled with action. Loving the West—particularly Western films—as I did, appearing in *Kit Carson* was a real thrill.

However, the role did lead to two unpleasant incidents. The first occurred while my family visited me in Tuba City, Arizona. They had driven out from Chicago in my father's Cadillac, and I was driving them around, showing them the scenery. I still have no recollection of how it happened, but the car slid off the highway and rolled over. By a wonderful stroke of luck, we rolled into a soft embankment, so no one was hurt. But it certainly shook us up.

Later, back in Hollywood, the second unpleasant incident occurred. Pleased with my new contract, I had sent for my father to come to California to visit me. I wanted to take my dad sport fishing. We chartered a boat and decided we would spend the night on it to get a very early start the next morning. Just before I went to bed, I told my father that I would like to get a bowl of soup before I retired, so I went to a little cafe on the wharf. In the cafe, three longshoremen—*drunk* longshoremen—were sitting near the entrance to the door. Because we were still shooting scenes for *Kit Carson*, I had long hair. Plus I was wearing a powder blue coat. They snickered as I walked past them. I sat down about halfway down the counter, had my bowl of soup and some crackers, and then got up and started to walk out. I was about to pay for the soup when I heard one of the longshoremen mutter, "Hey, look at the long hair on that guy!" I had a feeling there was going to be trouble.

Now I was in pretty good shape. I weighed 185 or 190 pounds, and worked out all the time. Two of the men were staring at me, so I kept an eye on them. But just as I paid the check and started to walk out, the third fellow on the bar stool swung around and nailed me, hitting me right in the face. I went down. All three of them went outside. There was no way to avoid the situation, so I took a deep breath and followed them out. All three longshoremen came at me at once. I decked two of them, nailed 'em pretty good, but the third caught me again in the eye. Then they got up and ran off. A sailor came by and offered to help. Of course, it was a little late for him to help me fight those three thugs, but I asked him to help me get back to the boat—I was pretty dazed. He took me to the boat, I awakened my father, and we left the boat and went to a hotel. My father called a doctor who checked my eye, and that was it.

Those three men had taken one look at my hair and coat and figured they could have a little fun—but they found out a little differently. I think I did pretty well for myself under the circumstances.

However, I had quite a shiner on my eye. In fact, it still tingles to this day because a nerve on my face was injured in that fight. Eddie Small had to hold the picture up for about a week, until I could be photographed again. There's a kind of an odd coincidence connected with that brawl. The doctor who treated my eye was married to an actress who later appeared with me in *The Lone Ranger and The Lost City of Gold*—eighteen years later.

⋈

My friendship with Lupe Velez was purely platonic. But, being a young single fellow in the prime of life, I was interested in forming *other* kinds of relationships. I met Mary Francis, a dancer and aspiring actress, at a party one weekend. She had come out to Los Angeles with George White's *Scandals*, a legendary stage revue. She did a dancing act with Andy Hall, the wife of Huntz Hall of the Bowery Boys and the Dead End Kids. Mary and I hit it off right away. At the end of the party, she asked me to give her a ride home. We became very serious about each other quickly. So quickly, in fact, that we decided to put the brakes on and make sure that we weren't rushing into anything.

One columnist caught wind of our unusual plan and wrote, "They are aware that many a Hollywood first sight romance has not stood the test of time, so they determined to ensure their affections before going to the altar. Miss Francis and Moore agreed not to see or communicate with each other for three months. If they decided they were still in love at the end of that time they would be married. The ninety day period expired at midnight last Thursday and at 12:01 Friday, Moore telephoned Miss Francis and said, 'Let's get married.'" We should have waited longer.

We got married in Las Vegas. A friend of mine arranged with Robert Perick, a man who supplied airplanes for the studios, to fly us there. Mary's mother came along, and she and Perick acted as our witnesses. We were married at about ten minutes to six on the afternoon of August 19, 1940, by Justice of the Peace George Marshall. Mary was eighteen and I was twenty-five.

This was during the period when I was going with Lupe.

When I told her about my marriage, she gave me her sincerest congratulations and said, "It couldn't happen to a nicer person."

The Monday after our wedding, Mary and I went to Denver for the world premiere of *Kit Carson*.

Mary and I lived on Peck Drive and Roxbury in an apartment building which was owned by, of all people, Charles Boyer's valet. I was already living there when we married; Mary just moved in. Most of my pals were still bachelors, but they were happy for me. They had their own clique, and after I got married, I wasn't in the clique anymore. I was a stay-at-home, married man. I bought Mary a little dog, Taffy, and a used Ford so she could get around on her own. She wanted to start taking dramatic lessons, and I paid for those, too.

It's hard to say what went wrong with our marriage, but it started going sour almost immediately. We lived together only a few months and were divorced in well under a year. We were both young and focused on our careers. Maybe that's what killed the marriage. Whatever it was, Mary soon moved out. I stayed in the apartment on Peck Drive—and I kept the dog Taffy.

After the divorce, I got a call from Mary one day, demanding that I return Taffy to her. I said, "Come on over. We'll let Taffy decide."

I was sitting on the couch when Mary arrived. Taffy was sitting there beside me. I was very friendly, but Mary wanted to get right down to business.

"Taffy," she called very sweetly, bending toward the dog. "Come here, baby."

Taffy just sat beside me, staring at Mary.

"Taffy!" A little less sweetly. "Come on." She even whistled a little.

Still, Taffy just sat there.

Mary stood straight up. "Get over here!"

This time Taffy snarled and bared his teeth. I took out my checkbook and wrote Mary a check for twenty-five dollars, exactly what we paid for the dog in the first place. I got up and gave her the check, and she turned around and walked out. I never saw her again.

$$\bowtie$$

Encouraged by my work in *Kit Carson*, Eddie Small made sure I got better roles in *The Son of Monte Cristo* (1940), a swashbuckler sequel to *The Count of Monte Cristo*, directed by Rowland V. Lee and starring Louis Hayward and Joan Bennett; and *International Lady* (1941), a spy picture with George Brent, Basil Rathbone, and Ilona Massey, and directed by Tim Whelan. I also learned a great deal by watching these great actors work. I wasn't taking dramatic classes anymore, but I still wanted to constantly improve myself and become a better actor.

After *International Lady*, Eddie Small was going to do a movie called *The Corsican Brothers*, which Gregory Ratoff was going to direct. Eddie called me into the office and said he wanted me to go down and see Ratoff for a part in this movie. So I called Ratoff's office and made an appointment with him. He had seen my work in *Kit Carson* and *International Lady* and seemed to know a great deal about me. He even knew about the leading role I didn't get in *South of Pago Pago*.

I asked him "What do you have in mind for me in *The Corsican Brothers*?"

Ratoff said, "Well, I'll tell you, I haven't got your part written yet. But I am thinking of something."

That struck me as a little odd. Just about the same time, my agent called and said that the casting director at Republic Studios would like to talk to me about a part. It was not a definite job offer, but I weighed the possibility of going to Republic Studios against a nonexistent part in Gregory Ratoff's *Corsican Brothers* and decided to take my chance with Republic. I went immediately to see Eddie Small and said, "Mr. Small, I would like my release." It didn't seem to surprise or bother him much. He just said, "That's all right Clayton, you can have your release."

And so I went to Republic Pictures.

CHAPTER FOUR

Republic Pictures

Republic Pictures was still one of Hollywood's newest studios when I arrived there in 1942. Herbert J. Yates formed Republic in 1935 by merging several "Poverty Row" film studios. Yates was an ambitious businessman who knew how to find a niche in the market and exploit it. In those days the major studios like MGM, Warner Bros., and Paramount owned their own chains of movie theaters, so they could control not only the production but the distribution of their films.

Independent theaters were usually found in rural areas or middle class city neighborhoods. They relied on smaller studios to supply them with movies. In the period before television, millions of Americans went to the movies every week, sometimes more than once. Where today a hit movie might play for weeks or even months, in those days the programs were changed up to twice a week. Yates figured that he could make a fortune by supplying these independent theaters with plenty of product, feature films, short subjects and serials. Republic wouldn't produce big budget "prestige" films like the big companies. Instead, Yates would make fast-paced, audience-pleasing entertainments: adventures, Westerns, and comedies.

Yates's idea worked. Republic's low-budget pictures almost always turned a healthy profit. More important, they were thoroughly enjoyed by the audiences who flocked to see them week after week.

I'll never forget the first day I walked through the gates of Republic Pictures. The studio was located on Ventura Boulevard, between Colfax and Radford in Studio City. (It is still there, by the way; now it's called CBS Television Center, and many top television programs are filmed on the old soundstages.) Back in the silent days, comic genius Mack Sennett had run the place, but now it was a Western paradise. Roy Rogers, Gene Autry, and John Wayne were Republic's biggest stars. I felt as though I had really come to the right place.

But it would be quite a while before I appeared in a Republic Western—a few years, in fact. The first movie I was cast in was *Tuxedo Junction* (1941). It was one of a series of rural musical comedies featuring characters called the Weaver Brothers and Elviry. These movies were a little like the *Ma and Pa Kettle* pictures over at Universal—good, clean family pictures, a little corny but very entertaining. Billie Benedict and Lorna Gray (who later changed her name to Adrian Booth) were also in *Tuxedo Junction*.

One of the stars of the film was a great character actor, Thurston Hall, who also appeared in Orson Welles's *Citizen Kane* the same year. The first day of the picture I was introduced to the cast, and when I met him I said, "It's nice to meet you, Mr. Hall."

He glowered at me and said, "I *hate* juveniles!"

I guess he just wanted to overpower me from the start.

It worked. I kept away from him throughout the entire production.

My next film was more exciting: *The Perils of Nyoka*[1]
(1942), a fifteen-part serial starring Kay Aldridge and directed by Republic's leading director, William Witney.

The character of Nyoka had first appeared in *Jungle Girl*
a year earlier, although in that serial she was played by
Frances Gifford. My pal Tom Neal played the male lead in
Jungle Girl. In *The Perils of Nyoka*, I was cast as Larry, the hero
who helps Nyoka battle the evil Vultura (Lorna Gray again)
while trying to discover the magical Golden Tablets of
Hippocrates. These tablets were the key to fabulous treasure,
but they also held secrets that could help doctors cure all
diseases. Nyoka and Larry, of course, wanted to use the
tablets for good, while Vultura was only after the treasure.

As directed by William Witney, *The Perils of Nyoka* was
exciting and entertaining. Bill was wonderful to work with,
considerate, good with action. He never had to ask the
script girl what scene was to be shot next—he was sharp,
organized, knew the script like the back of his hand. Bill
always knew exactly where the camera should be set up
and how the scene should be played. I guess he did a lot
of homework.

Bill Witney was terrific with the actors, too. He used to
kid Kay Aldridge about her accent—she had a little Texas
twang, not quite what you'd expect from a jungle princess.
She took it all in the spirit of fun and kidded Bill right back.
Scripts for serials were very, very long—two or three inches
thick—and we had to work at a very quick pace. But Bill was
the kind of director who knew that the cast and crew had to

---

[1] *The Perils of Nyoka's* title was later changed to *Nyoka and the Tigermen*,
and that's the title under which you'll find the serial on home video.

relax and have a little fun now and then. As hard as we worked on *The Perils of Nyoka*, I don't remember feeling as though we were under unbearable pressure. It was a hard job, but an enjoyable one.

Movie making at Republic was as efficient as possible. With such low budgets, we didn't have the luxury of doing take after take. You had to be awfully good at your job, memorize your lines, know your business, because if you wanted your performance to come across, you'd only get one shot at it. Everyone there was professional in the extreme, knowing exactly what they had to do at all times. I admired that attitude. We all pitched in to make the picture as good as we possibly could.

We worked from eight in the morning until the sun went down. Sometimes we would break for dinner and then go back to work overtime. The pace could be exhausting, but we never felt as though the studio was taking advantage of us. We loved doing the job.

I learned a great deal about movie making on the set of *The Perils of Nyoka*. When I walked on the set the very first day, two stuntmen, Dave Sharpe and Tom Steele, were spinning guns, practicing drawing and spinning. I had just been given my outfit and gun belt, and as I walked past them, I twirled my gun and threw a fan shot at Dave. I guess they didn't think too much of that because I got the silent treatment for a week. Of course, I was young, it was my first lead in a serial, and I was showing off a little.

Pretty soon, though, we were the best of friends. Dave, Tom, and all the other stuntmen were kind to me and taught me how to stage a fight and take a fall. They thought of me as one of the guys because I was so interested in athletics and physical stunts. I think I was a pretty good pupil, too. Dave Sharpe was my stunt double on *The Perils of Nyoka*, but after that, Tom Steele took over and doubled me through all the serials I did at Republic. Sometimes he acted in the serials, too.

Tom would go on to teach me everything about stunts: fighting, gun twirling, horseback riding, rearing shots—although I really didn't start rearing horses until *The Lone Ranger's* Silver. *The Perils of Nyoka*, in fact, is actually the very first time I ever did action horseback riding in a movie. However, I later revised my riding style. If you watch *The Perils of Nyoka*, you'll notice that I rode with the reins high. On *The Lone Ranger* and other Westerns, I preferred holding the reins down, near the horse. There is one rearing shot in *The Perils of Nyoka* where the horse almost came over backwards. That was a bit hairy, but that's how you learn.

A stable behind Warner Bros. was where Tom Steele and I did all our gun twirling and horse training. He taught me crouper mounts, running-start mounts, everything. In a running-start mount, you run, leap toward the horse, put your foot in the stirrup, and mount—you do the whole thing on the run. A crouper mount is when you leap over the back end of the horse (the back part of the horse is called a croup) and land in the saddle. And, of course, rearing is when the horse stands on hind legs and paws the air with front legs. This is what I always did with Silver in *The Lone Ranger's* main titles. The horses were well trained for all this action. In some of the Republic films I rode John Wayne's horse Banner.

One of the highlights of *The Perils of Nyoka* is when I have a fight with a giant gorilla. A very talented man, Emil Van Horn, played the ape, and it was fascinating to hear him describe how he made his own costume from a combination of leather and real hair. He created a voice box that fit inside the ape mask, and Van Horn told me that to make sure that he really sounded authentic, he often went to the zoo, spending hours studying gorillas' actions and sounds.

He did his job very well. In fact, when our fight scene started, I got the oddest feeling. Just for a fraction of a second, I felt a tingle of real fear up my spine—I thought, that's a real gorilla! The studio knew how valuable Van Horn was, too. After Dave Sharpe, Van Horn was the highest paid performer in *The Perils of Nyoka*. He got $300 a week.

I met Tristram Coffin on the set of *The Perils of Nyoka*, too. He was a wonderful character actor who often played in Republic, Monogram, and other low-budget studios' films and serials. He told me that he had been one of the radio reporters covering the kidnapping of the Lindbergh baby a few years earlier. Tris and I worked together often over the course of our careers; we became close friends. A few years later, he would be cast as my older brother, Dan Reid, in the opening episode of *The Lone Ranger*.

The Perils of Nyoka was filmed from March 20 to May 2, 1942. To get so much footage in so little time, the people at Republic always planned the production in minute detail. We would go to a single location and shoot every scene that was set there, then move on to our next location. I suppose that editing these scenes into fifteen chapters was a little like putting a jigsaw puzzle together. We filmed all the exteriors of *Nyoka* at Iverson's Ranch, where most of *The Lone Ranger* episodes would be shot later. The place where we filmed is still there and very recognizable. Because of the rough terrain, they couldn't build condominiums in that area in later years. One sharp incline became known as the *Perils of Nyoka* cliff; it was used in so many Republic shows. Every morning we would meet at Republic Studios in Studio City, get into our costumes, and then be driven up to the location.

Of course, we all had to learn to work with difficult, temperamental actors, and I worked with one of the most temperamental on *The Perils of Nyoka*—Georgie, the monkey. Georgie was, to put it mildly, a little jumpy. When we were working on the soundstage, if he did something wrong or things didn't work out right, he would squeal loudly and climb up the side of the stage to the catwalk. His trainer would have to coax him down. Everything stopped until they got Georgie back in the scene. Georgie was a real prima donna. He liked Bill Witney, though. I guess he knew which side his bread was buttered on.

Fang the dog, however, was a thorough professional and a delight to work with.

Although I did several more serials in my career, *The Perils of Nyoka* remains my favorite. It was just such fun to do and the people I worked with were interesting and friendly. I think if you watch *The Perils of Nyoka* today, you'll find that a lot of that excitement and good-natured fun worked its way onto the screen. In fact, I heard that Steven Spielberg watched this serial when he was planning *Raiders of the Lost Ark*. I don't know if this is true, but it wouldn't surprise me a bit.

}∞{

At around the time we were filming *Perils*, my pal Tom Neal invited me to a party at his house in Playa Del Ray. I went there with Lupe Velez. I remember that, because we were planning on swimming at the party, Lupe gave me a pair of Johnny Weissmuller's white swimming trunks. We were having a great time when I noticed a beautiful young woman who had come to the party with a group of friends. Her name was Sally Allen, and she had moved to California from Minneapolis several years earlier. She had been married once, to Jack Allen, a music shop owner. I didn't know it at the time, but she had also been involved with John Barrymore, who was a great deal older than she was. I got Tom to introduce me.

Sally told me she occasionally did some stand-in and extra work in the movies. She even did a bit part now and then. "I don't think I'm cut out to be an actress," she said smiling. "Every time I get in front of the camera, I can never get through a line without laughing."

"You laugh because you're nervous?" I asked.

"No," Sally said. "I just think it's kind of silly, so I burst into laughter."

I must say it was kind of a relief to meet a beautiful young woman who wasn't particularly interested in a career in the movies. I was intrigued by Sally, but also delighted by her. She had a wonderful sense of humor and laughed easily and often. And she was very beautiful. I thought she was wonderful.

If she had decided to take acting seriously, Sally probably could have been one of the best. She had personality to spare—and Hollywood connections most people would kill for. Although she wasn't exactly a celebrity (one columnist wrote, "She looks more like a movie star than the movie stars do"), Sally's name popped up repeatedly in gossip columns, such as Louella Parsons. These tidbits could range from the fact that her dog Queenie had recently had six puppies to Sally's "engagement" to some local Romeo or other. Like me, Sally had been a model—although I must say she looked much better in a bathing suit than I did. But she really made her mark on Hollywood when she began her relationship with the great actor John Barrymore. In 1937, the gossip columns were filled with speculation about just who this new "mystery woman" in Barrymore's life was. Although the two of them always denied publicly that they were a romantic item, most observers believe that Barrymore had fallen in love with Sally—and who could blame him? Their pictures certainly ended up in the papers often enough, dining at Ciro's or the Pirate's Den or taking in the races at Santa Anita. Hollywood had a particular aura of glamour in those days, and Sally enjoyed every minute of it.

I was next cast in *The Black Dragons* (1942), a wartime thriller about a Nazi doctor (Bela Lugosi) who performs plastic surgery on Japanese spies to help them infiltrate the American military. He turns them into exact duplicates of six powerful Americans, then murders the Americans. It was farfetched, of course, but exciting. Maybe it seemed a little less farfetched at the time because we were really starting a war with Germany and Japan and American audiences were nervous about the future.

It was a great thrill for me to work with Bela Lugosi. As a kid, I loved *Dracula* and was familiar with all of his horror pictures. Of course, he was nothing like the roles he played. Instead, Lugosi was very polite and reserved; he stayed pretty much to himself. He wasn't unfriendly; he just wasn't very talkative.

Lugosi was also well rehearsed and meticulous. If you changed a word of dialog, he would go over and sit in a chair, read through the script, and add the line at the appropriate place. He didn't react well if you just asked him to change something on the spur of the moment. Lugosi was a fine actor, I know that, and nice to work with.

Black Dragons was produced at Monogram Studios, a real low-budget outfit. But I never considered the low budgets a negative. I always felt that if you couldn't throw a lot of money at a problem, you had to solve it with ingenuity and creativity. William Nigh, the director, had already been making movies for over thirty years—even in 1942—and he always had an inventive way of shooting a scene so that the viewers wouldn't notice the sparse sets or other defects. These were important lessons for me to learn because working in television in the fifties would offer the same kinds of challenges we were facing every day on the sets of movies like *Black Dragons*—too little time, too little money, but the show must go on.

After *Black Dragons* I looked forward to my next movie assignment, but Uncle Sam had other plans for me. I learned even before production on *Black Dragons* was completed that my next performance might be in the theater of war.

I had been drafted.

CHAPTER FIVE

In the Army Now

A t first it was kind of a shock to realize that I was going to have to leave home and my movie work—and Sally Allen—to go off and serve my country. But the shock soon turned to pride. I've always been very grateful to live in the United States, and I considered it an honor to be able to do something important for this country.

Times were different then, too. Nearly everyone in the country fully supported our military actions overseas. We all felt that Germany and Japan had started the war, and it was up to the Allied forces to make sure that the world was made safe for democracy.

I was assigned to the army air force and, after my induction, was shipped off to Sheppard Field, Texas, for my basic training. However, because of my bad knee from the trampoline accident, I was not allowed to go overseas to fight.

One morning at about four o'clock, we were all lined up for overseas medical shots. I told the sergeant, as respectfully as possible, that I wasn't going overseas because of my trick knee, so I didn't need to get the shots. He scanned the list on his clipboard.

"You're John C. Moore?" he asked

I replied, "Yes, I'm John C. Moore."

"Well, you're on the list."

"But I'm not supposed to be," I said. "I'm not going overseas."

The sergeant was not impressed. He stalked away, and I continued to stand there in line.

Eventually the line snaked into the infirmary. I could see up ahead that men were receiving painful shots with huge, ugly needles. Now I don't mind getting a shot if I have to, but I sure didn't see any reason to go through this.

An officer came walking by. "Excuse me, sir," I said. He stopped. "I'm not supposed to be here, sir. I'm in the limited service and I'm not set up for overseas duty."

"What's your name?" he asked.

"John C. Moore, sir," I said. He left to get a list, looked it over, then came back.

"You're on the list," he said.

I couldn't seem to make anyone understand that I wasn't *supposed* to be on the list.

Finally, I got nearer to the front of the line. There was a lieutenant on one side and a sergeant on the other, and I was supposed to get a shot in both arms. There must have been fifteen or twenty fellows in front of me, and the officers were reading off the names. When they came to my name, I said, "That's me, but you can check my record. I'm not supposed to be here."

The lieutenant sighed and asked me to spell my name. I did, "*J O H N C M O O R E.*"

He looked closely at the list. "Oh," he said. "That explains it. The name on the list is 'John Seymour.' You're dismissed, soldier."

As I passed the sergeant who had given me such a rough time earlier, I said, "You know, there are two animals that have stripes, skunks and sergeants." He was not amused. I was immediately put on KP duty for two weeks, peeling thousands of potatoes by hand. After that, I had a new nickname around Sheppard Field: Joe Spud.

After basic training, I was shipped to the air force base in Kingman, Arizona, and placed in Special Services. We were in charge of entertainment, putting on shows. Sometimes we mounted comedy water shows—silly dives off the diving board—and other times we did musical revues or plays. My Special Service Unit also coordinated the various USO shows that came through. A lot of top Hollywood talent, like band leader Kay Kyser, would come around to entertain the troops in those days. That was lucky for us—Kingman was pretty isolated.

We also could go into the town of Kingman and see movies. One time I was surprised to see *Tuxedo Junction* playing there. My friend Frank Ellerbrook had arranged a special screening just for the soldiers out at the base. He acted as master of ceremonies, and the guys really applauded when I came onscreen. I don't think it changed my status or anything, but it was fun to share some of my former life with my new buddies.

In the weeks before I had to report for service, Sally and I had fallen very much in love. Now we were separated by hundreds of miles. She was contributing to the war effort by working in an aircraft factory at Douglas Air Force Base (Sally the Riveter!) during the day and entertaining at an officers' club in the evenings. The officers' club was modeled on the famous Hollywood Canteen. It offered servicemen a place to go have a meal and see a show, and all the Hollywood stars would come and help out.

Of course, I missed Sally very much. Every Saturday night, Frank Ellerbrook and I would go into Kingman and call our sweethearts on the telephone. This went on for several months until Sally and I agreed that we were sick of being separated. So one Saturday night, I introduced a new subject into the conversation. I asked her to marry me.

She didn't answer me right away, saying that she wanted to think about it. She talked it over with her roommate Dolores who said, "You love Clay, don't you?"

Sally said she did.

"Then," Dolores said, "why not marry him?"

The next Saturday night when I called, Sally told me that she would be my wife.

I only had $900. I sent it to her and told her to buy a trailer. The next time I had a few days' furlough, I drove back to Hollywood in my 1940 Mercury, hitched the little sixteen-foot trailer to it, and Sally and I drove back to Kingman. We were married a few days later at the Kingman City Hall and lived in the Park Lane Trailer Park. We never stayed at the post.

Living in a small trailer with a little canvas house attached to it wasn't the most luxurious way to spend a honeymoon, especially for Sally, who had given up her posh life in Beverly Hills to "rough it" with me out in the middle of nowhere. But she was a real trooper, and she made life in that tiny trailer fun and exciting. Sally and I were young and in love, and we knew that things would get better once the war was over. Besides, most of the people who lived in the trailer park were officers in the air force, so Sally had the other wives to keep her company; however, I was an enlisted man, and officers were discouraged from mixing with enlisted men, so we didn't have much of a social life with other nearby couples. While I was at work on the base, Sally took care of our two dogs—Dale, her springer spaniel, and Taffy, my cocker spaniel. Taffy really loved Sally. We also put on a show for the officers in the officers' club in Kingman in 1943.

A few months after we were married, I transferred from Special Services to plane dispatching. It was my job to figure out the different missions for the pilots every day.

All in all, things were going very well for us. Sally and I were happy, and I had grown used to life in the air force. I was a little worried about what awaited me back home— would I be able to pick up my movie career where I had left off almost two years earlier? I stayed in touch with my friend Tom Neal but otherwise had virtually no contact with Hollywood.

Then came the darkest day of this entire period. One evening in 1944 I received word that my father had passed away. He and I had always been very close, and I admired and respected him. I took his death hard. Sally and I flew to Chicago for his funeral. That sad occasion also turned out to be one of the last times I ever saw my older brother Sprague. He died in 1946.

In early 1945 I was transferred from Kingman to the motion picture unit in Culver City. Both Sally and I were delighted that we could go back home where life could become somewhat normal again. I worked on training films there. I remember one scene where I was in an airplane doing a little technical radar. It wasn't exactly like being back on the set at Republic, but at least I was one step closer to returning to my real profession. I fell ill that summer and was hospitalized in Santa Ana, California. The war was virtually over by then, and so I was given an honorable discharge in Santa Ana on July 5, 1945.

It was good to be a civilian again, even though I wasn't sure what my next move would be. I had my agent contact Republic to find out if I could come back and resume my contract. In the meantime, I had to earn some money. All discharged GIs were on what we called the "52-20 plan," which meant that we would receive twenty dollars every week for a year. Even with the value of the dollar in 1945, you couldn't live on twenty dollars a week, though it was a great help.

Sally and I were also able to obtain a GI loan to start building a modest house in Santa Monica. If you want an indication of how times have changed, consider that our house and the lot cost us $7,000. Just try buying a Santa Monica home for that price these days. The builder's name was Miles Thomas, and when he learned that we could use extra money, he hired Sally and me. I helped dig foundations and scraped the paint off walls and windows. Sally would be inside the house with a razor paint scraper, and she would clean the windows, tubs, and sinks after the walls were plastered and plaster was spattered everywhere. I would also build fences and burn scrap lumber. In short, we would do everything possible to get a house ready for occupancy. Sally and I earned fifteen dollars per house. It was hard work, but both of us enjoyed being physical. We would tie Dale and Taffy outside, and at lunch time we would have a little picnic in the yard.

Just like almost every soldier, we had a brief period of struggling when I first got out of the service. But then, with our new house and our happy marriage, life seemed good indeed. We were healthy and active, and if we weren't rich, at least we weren't poor. Besides, things were looking up in that area, too: I was once again working steadily in the movies— back at Republic Pictures.

CHAPTER SIX

King of the B's

I had gotten a kick out of my first Republic serial, *The Perils of Nyoka*, before the war, so I was truly thrilled at the prospect of getting back to the studio with all my old friends and working on more cliffhangers. Because they were intended for juvenile audiences at Saturday matinees, I don't think our serials ever earned much respect from the motion picture industry. But fans loved them, they were consistently profitable, and those of us who performed in them enjoyed the work. I considered them a great training ground where I would learn about acting, riding, shooting, special effects—everything involved in making motion pictures.

Republic had been making serials since *Darkest Africa* (1936). From then until 1955 (*King of the Carnival*), the studio would make sixty-six cliffhangers. The serials consisted of twelve to fifteen chapters, each lasting about fifteen minutes. If run from first chapter to last, they would measure as short as 167 minutes or as long as 290 minutes. Either way, a serial used up much more footage and running time than any Republic feature film, but the shooting schedules were just as short, usually about four weeks.

The kids who loved the Republic cliffhangers in the thirties and forties continued to love them as adults. While today the great majority of my fans think of me primarily as the Lone Ranger, there is an avid minority more interested in my career as a serial star. That's fine with me. My stay at Republic Pictures was among the most exciting and rewarding (creatively, not financially) of my career. In fact, every once in a while I watch one of the old serials on video, and you know what? They're still as much fun as they ever were: lively, fast-paced, imaginative—and sometimes downright strange. The plots were filled with dangerous robots, exotic undersea kingdoms, cunning spies, super heroes, and flying men. In other words, the world of the serial was not very much like real life. Maybe that's why they were so incredibly popular throughout the dark years of the Great Depression and World War II.

The Crimson Ghost [2] (1946), with Charles Quigley and Linda Stirling, was the first serial I appeared in after getting out of the army. Nearly four years had passed since we'd made *The Perils of Nyoka*, but working with many of the same actors and crew made it feel like old home week. Freddy Brannon had been a prop man the last time I saw him. Now he was codirecting *The Crimson Ghost* with Bill Witney, the director of *Nyoka*.

My pal Tom Steele was now acting as my stunt double. My hair was thick and black, but Tom's was light and he was nearly bald, so he had to wear a dark wig whenever he doubled me. Things were pretty slapdash sometimes. When I watch *The Crimson Ghost* today, it amazes me that sometimes you can see Tom's bald head quite clearly—even though he's supposed to be me. I'm really surprised no one caught it. Or maybe they did and just didn't care.

The Crimson Ghost was the first time I played a bad guy

---

[2] A feature-length edited version of *The Crimson Ghost* is available on video under the title *Cyclotrode "X."*

or "heavy" and I enjoyed the experience tremendously. In those days the hero always had to speak and behave properly, but the villain could relax a little, use slang, smoke a cigarette. It was just more fun being bad. I played Ashe, one of the Crimson Ghost's henchman. The Crimson Ghost was actually played by two actors—Stan Jolly wore the costume throughout the serial, but when it came time to be unmasked, the Crimson Ghost was played by Joe Forte. My scenes with that evil character were some of the most difficult to perform—we kept breaking up. Even though we were supposed to be serious and ominous, it was pretty hard to keep a straight face when looking the Crimson Ghost in the eye.

Because of the mask, the sound men had a hard time picking up the Crimson Ghost's dialog. They inserted a voice box, but even that sometimes made the speech hard to understand. I believe a great deal of the character's dialog had to be dubbed later.

As usual, we went out to Iverson's Ranch for most of the location work. In those days we had to park our cars at a gas station on the corner of Devonshire and Topanga Canyon, and take a bus up to Iverson's. The unions wouldn't let actors drive onto the Ranch for insurance reasons. We shot those thrilling car chases on the winding Malibu Canyon and Topanga Canyon Roads. Some sections still look the same today as they did then, wild and beautiful.

Otherwise, the whole serial was filmed right there on the Republic back lot—you can also see the studio's administration building. The famous Republic Cave was used of course. The cave showed up in nearly every Republic serial and many features. It was rented out to other studios, too. I often thought that Republic head Herbert Yates probably made more money on that cave than he did on his pictures.

The fight scenes in these serials always had to be planned carefully. That wasn't only for safety—after all, we were only actors—but because if it had to be shot again, all that broken furniture would have to be replaced, and that could run into real money. Republic's method was one take, whenever possible. The stuntmen would perform the entire fight at once and our close-ups would be added later.

Of course, when there's an animal involved, one take isn't always possible. In chapter 11 of *The Crimson Ghost*, a dog was supposed to chase the ghost. Although they tried take after take, the dog just wasn't interested. Finally his trainer put on the Crimson Ghost's costume and ran across the set, the dog tearing out after him—in one take.

In my next serial, there was a stunt that I decided to do myself—and later wished that I hadn't. For a scene in *Jesse James Rides Again* (1947), I was supposed to drive a hay wagon that had been set on fire. Just before the wagon was to hit a rock and overturn, I was supposed to leap off and roll away. The leap went fine. Then the wagon hit the rock and overturned. The bad part was that it overturned *toward* me, missing me by only a few inches. After that, I turned the big stunts back over to Tom Steele.

Although Jesse James was a historical character, there was nothing authentic about the story we told. In *Jesse James Rides Again*, Jesse is trying to reform and work his Missouri farm. But when he learns that he is going to be arrested for a bank robbery in which he didn't take part, he heads south. There he gets involved with farmers who are being attacked by masked raiders who want the oil on their land. Jesse helps to save the day and, in the process, clears his name.

Obviously the real Jesse James was a vicious outlaw, a

Sprague C. and Theresa Violet Moore, my parents, in 1935.

The Moore boys *(left to right)*, Sprague, Howard, and Clayton, in 1925.

In 1925 I saddled up behind my brother Howard on the first—but not the last—white horse I ever rode.

My father on one of the family's fishing expeditions in the twenties. This beauty weighed 17 ½ pounds.

The Flying Behrs

Practicing with the Flying Behrs for the 1934 Chicago World's Fair (I'm on the far left above, standing on the bar below).

I fly through the air with the greatest of ease at the 1934
World's Fair in Chicago.

Up-and-coming actors in their underwear in California. *(Left to right)* Rand
Brooks, me, Tom Neal, Eddie Polo in 1938.

Mom, Dad, and Howard visit the set of *Kit Carson* in August of 1940 and meet supporting actress Renie Riano.

My future wife Sally Allen with "The Great Profile"—John Barrymore, May 1937.

Lupe Velez and I compare muscle
tone for a 1930s layout in *Photoplay*
Magazine.

Lupe Velez—the Mexican Spitfire

Sally Allen entertains W. C.
Fields and crooner Rudy
Vallee at the opening of the
Pirate's Den nightspot in
May 1940.

Sally and me at our engagement
party in 1943.

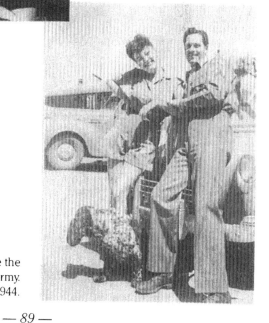

Sally, myself, and Dale the
spaniel in the army.
Kingman, Arizona, 1944.

On the set of *Kit Carson* in Flagstaff, Arizona, June 1940.

I sport a sarong for
South of Pago Pago
(1940)—a role I didn't
get to play.

I'm standing just behind Basil Rathbone *(second from right)* in *International Lady* (1941).

Fights in the serials were well choreographed, but they could still be pretty rough. Here I'm slugging it out in *G-Men Never Forget* (1947).

Bela Lugosi, Joan Barclay, and myself in *Black Dragons* (1942).

Linda Stirling and I meet the mysterious title character in *The Crimson Ghost* (1946).

Kay Aldridge and I struggle with Kenny Terrel in a cliff-hanging scene from *The Perils of Nyoka* (1942).

Kay Aldridge, me, and Emil Van Horn in a gorilla suit for *The Perils of Nyoka* (1942).

Even through the mask, my blue eyes shine in *The Ghost of Zorro* (1949). This is the film that won the role of The Lone Ranger for me.

A dynamite explosion that proved almost too realistic from *The Ghost of Zorro* (1949).

I nearly get creamed by a burning wagon in *Jesse James Rides Again* (1947).

Commando Cody (George Wallace) gets the drop on me *(second from left)* and other interplanetary bad guys in *Radar Men from the Moon* (1952).

Bad guys never win in a Roy Rogers movie! Here, Roy gets the best of me in *The Far Frontier* (1949).

And you don't want to tangle with Gene Autry, either! Here I am getting pummeled by Gene in *The Cowboy and the Indians* (1949). As this picture makes clear, I frequently did my own stunts.

Jay Silverheels and I worked in the same scene—but never met—in *The Cowboy and the Indians* (1949). I'm standing between Jay *(in headband)* and Gene Autry.

Here I am *(far left)* with my pal Rand Brooks *(far right)* in *The Son of Monte Cristo* (1940). Second from left is star Louis Hayward.

I got to portray another Western legend in *Buffalo Bill in Tomahawk Territory* (1952). I'm seen here with Chief Yolachie.

Sally, Silver, and me—unmasked—on the set of a Lone Ranger episode in 1949.

Who was that goofy man? That's me in May 1947.

I'm acting demure at a surprise party in my Tarzana home, celebrating my 35th birthday, September 14, 1949. The very first episode of *The Lone Ranger* debuted the next day.

bank robber and killer, but audiences didn't seem to mind that we turned him into a sympathetic, law-abiding character. After all, it was only a serial and a very exciting one at that. And *I* sure didn't mind. Not only was I playing the lead, but at last I was appearing in a Western. Only a few years earlier I had been sitting in the Granada Theater, dreaming of riding the range, having shoot-outs, and doing all the other exciting things that I saw Tom Mix and William S. Hart doing. Nothing is as thrilling as having a dream come true—and I enjoyed every minute of it.

Of course, I always took my leading roles with a grain of salt. It seemed to me that the only requirements for getting a lead in a Republic serial were that you read dialogue, be in strong physical condition, and closely resemble at least one of the stuntmen.

I learned a lot on the set of *Jesse James Rides Again*. It was only the second time I had ridden a horse on screen (after *The Perils of Nyoka*), and I wasn't very good at it. The Hudkins brothers, Ace and Ode, furnished Republic's horse stock, and this is the picture on which I rode John Wayne's horse Banner. Lucky for me, Banner was a lot more professional at this than I was; he made me look pretty good. Watching this serial today, I'm slightly embarrassed by how much I talk to the horse—"Whoa!" or "Ho!" or "Giddap!" I soon learned that true horsemen signal their horse with reins and spurs, not voice commands, but at this early date, I was still an amateur. Banner was patient, however, and tried his best to teach me the ropes.

During the filming of *Jesse James Rides Again*, I learned to do a jump mount that I used later quite often on *The Lone Ranger*. To do it, you use the saddle horn to get yourself up in the air, then stab the stirrup with your foot. Tom Steele taught me how to do this—we spent hour after hour practicing at the Hudkin brothers' place. It was hard work, but I had the time of my life. I would have worked for free—in fact, considering what Republic paid me, I almost did. I got paid around $200 a week for appearing in these serials. I believe the biggest money I ever got at Republic was $450 a week.

Even from the beginning, I was careful about keeping track of how many bullets I used during a shoot-out. It always bothered me to see someone fire seven or eight shots from a six-shooter, so I kept strict count. Every time I fired my sixth bullet, I would reload. I learned another shoot-out trick, too. Sometimes the gun's report is so loud that it makes you blink when you fire it. That doesn't look good on film—a cowboy has to have that steely eyed glare in the close-up. I found that if I clenched a match or twig between my teeth, I wouldn't blink when I fired the gun.

Once, though, I did *more* than blink at a gunshot. I had an ear infection and wasn't feeling well. However, I didn't want to miss work, so I reported to the set anyway. Johnny Compton and I were doing a shooting scene together. He was at my right, and he was left-handed. I'd almost forgotten my ear infection until he pulled his gun and fired it inches from my ear. The pain was excruciating. I had to go straight to the studio doctor.

Roy Barcroft played one of the villains in *Jesse James Rides Again*. Roy played villains in more pictures than I can count. In real life, though, he couldn't have been less like the parts that he played. He was a big bear cub of a man. He and his wife Vera often had dinner with Sally and me. Roy and I didn't talk about show business much, but he once told me that he had patterned himself after Harry Woods, one of the movies' greatest villains. Woods had been the personification of evil as far back as *The Perils of Pauline* in 1914 and had snarled his way through any number of movie classics such as *The Plainsman* (1937), *Beau Geste* (1939), *Reap the Wild Wind* (1942), and—my favorite Western—*She Wore a Yellow Ribbon* (1949). I think Roy even tried to imitate Woods's voice—Roy sounded completely different on camera and off. Roy also loved motorcycles and usually rode his to the studio (Roy Rogers was quite a motorcycle rider, too; I used to see him speeding around the Republic back lot). I rode Roy's motorcycle up the street one time. But *just* once. I didn't care for it at all.

Linda Stirling was also wonderful to work with, so beautiful and talented. Known as "Queen of the Serials," she had been a popular star at Republic for several years. I believe *Jesse James Rides Again* was her last. She was engaged to Sloan Nibley during the filming and quit show business to marry him. I heard that she later became a teacher. I saw Linda in 1992 when we both appeared on Leonard Maltin's television special *The Cliffhangers*, and she looked terrific.

One of the things I remember about *G-Men Never Forget* (1947), my next serial, is that they asked me to provide my own clothes. I was always eager to make a good impression—I wanted to be hired again—so I was glad to bring in a few suits. Everybody used to buy clothes at MacIntosh on Hollywood Boulevard; if you watch *G-Men Never Forget*, you'll see exactly what the well-dressed man of 1947 was wearing.

G-Men Never Forget was an exciting gangster serial, and I played a real tough guy. I'll bet I was the only person on the set who had ever seen Al Capone in person. Freddy Brannon codirected the serial with the legendary stuntman Yakima Canutt. Canutt performed some of the great stunts in movie history. Remember that scene in John Ford's *Stagecoach* (1939) when John Wayne leaps off the stagecoach onto the horse team? That was Yak. So was the scene in the same movie when an Indian is shot off his horse, gets his foot caught in the stirrup, and is dragged along at top speed. Yak even acted in a whole series of B-Westerns at Republic and other studios. In *G-Men Never Forget*, Brannon directed most of the dramatic scenes, but Yak was in charge of the action—and nobody did it better.

Of course, stuntmen are a breed apart. Eddie Parker, who also worked on this serial, had been a mortician before he started doubling. He told me once—and swore it was true—that if he was burying someone in a tuxedo and he had a date that night, he would wear the tuxedo. He said, "What was the harm? My client wouldn't miss it for one night. After all, he's gonna be wearing it for a looong time!" I was flabbergasted. Once we heard the story, Roy Barcroft and I really gave Eddie the business. We never ran out of mortician jokes. He was a little odd, I grant you, but Eddie was a great stunt double.

Stuntman Dave Sharpe worked on nearly every Republic serial. I remember we were shooting a fire scene in *G-Men Never Forget*, and he was going to do a stunt that required him to fall out of the third story of a burning building. He was supposed to be caught by a fireman. Actually he was going to fall into a pile of cardboard boxes just out of camera range. We had a real fireman on the set to show Sharpe how to do the stunt authentically. Dave and I were sitting around waiting for the special effects people to get the fire set up properly when the fireman came over to Dave.

He said, "Young man, have you ever done anything like this before?"

Dave thought he would have a little fun with the man, so

he looked up at the third story window and gulped. "Oh my," he said, "that really looks so high up there!"

The fireman was kind of a know-it-all, puffing on a big cigar. "Look," he said to Dave, "there's nothing to it. You watch me and do exactly as I do and everything will come out fine." He was very condescending. It was all I could do to keep from breaking up, but I tried to look as worried as Dave did.

The fireman climbed up to the window and called down to Dave, "Are you watching?"

Dave was still acting nervous. "Oh goodness," he said, "it looks higher than ever!"

The fireman made the leap. He looked great coming down—but he missed the cardboard boxes and broke his leg.

As the fireman was being carried away on a stretcher, Dave went up to him and said, "Sir, I don't have to do it *exactly* that way, do I?"

I truly enjoyed working in serials, but I couldn't help but wonder if they were a sort of dead end. Few real movie stars started out in serials—John Wayne is a notable exception. It was almost as though, once the industry pegged you as a serial actor, they couldn't see you in any other light.

That's why I was always glad to get even minor roles in feature films. I got to play another villain in *Along the Oregon Trail* (1947), making life difficult for Monte Hale and Adrian Booth, and I had a small part in *Masked Raiders* (1949) with Tim Holt and Richard Martin.

I suppose that I conducted my movie career in a funny way. I never turned down a role. I wasn't concerned about screen time, billing, salary, or anything else. I just wanted to keep working, plain and simple. It never occurred to me to wonder whether this or that part was a good career move. I just liked working, regardless of whether I was the star or had seventh billing.

But even though I had roles in a few feature films, throughout this period, serials were my bread and butter. I returned to the character of Jesse James in *Adventures of Frank and Jesse James* (1948), which co-starred Steve Darrell and Noel Neill. Again Jesse was portrayed positively. In this serial he and his brother Frank want to make restitution to the people they robbed in the past, but of course, they run into all sorts of problems.

Noel Neill was a lovely young actress with a great deal of talent. She later went on to star as Lois Lane in the *Superman* television series with George Reeves. Like me, Noel was happy at Republic. (An interesting fact, I also appeared in a serial, *Jungle Drums of Africa* [1953], opposite Phyllis Coates, the *other* Lois Lane.)

I think everybody at Republic felt that we were part of a big happy family. The studio didn't have a glamorous reputation, but it remained my favorite place to work. Everyone was cooperative and willing to help you out at all times. The work was fast paced and interesting, and we always had fun on the set—even when we were working our hardest. I don't know how we had the energy to do all we did in those days, but I wouldn't trade my memories of Republic Pictures for anything.

Of course, there was no way to suspect this at the time, but my next serial would literally change the course of my life. I was given the lead in *The Ghost of Zorro* (1949), playing Ken Mason, an engineer from the East who turns out to be the grandson of the original Zorro, the masked Robin Hood figure of southern California. When Rita (Pamela Blake), the girl he loves, is threatened by George Crane (Roy Barcroft), the evil head of an outlaw empire, Ken dons the mask of Zorro and thwarts Crane's schemes.

The character of Zorro had been a screen favorite since Douglas Fairbanks starred in *The Mask of Zorro* back in 1920. Zorro was really big at Republic Pictures, where several Zorro serials were made including *Zorro Rides Again* (1937), *Zorro's Fighting Legion* (1939), *Zorro's Black Whip* (1944) and others. An odd coincidence, Bob Livingston played Zorro several years earlier, in *The Bold Caballero* (1937), just as he portrayed the Lone Ranger before I did.

The Ghost of Zorro was great fun to make, but there was one occasion when my pal Tom Steele didn't think it was so much fun. It happened during one of those rugged Republic fight scenes. We always blocked out our fights carefully, so that it would look nice and rough onscreen but would be relatively safe in reality. It was similar to choreographing a dance—when I step here, you move there. Usually the fights were left entirely to the stuntmen, but on this occasion we figured it would work best if I did it myself because the camera was going to be so close. Tom Steele and I worked out all of our business. The fight would climax with a dramatic fall over a bannister. Just before we did the take, Freddy Brannon, the director, said, "Make it look good, guys—real and tough!"

He called out. "Action!" Tom and I went to it, slugging away (and, of course, just missing each other as we swung our fists past each other's face); we knew that it was looking great. We had a code to signal that the fight was over—I would deliver a right, a left, and a right. We used to joke that it said *The End* across our knuckles. So we fought savagely, then I threw the right, left, and right, and Tom went plunging over the bannister.

Freddy called out, "Print it! Beautiful, fellas!" I started walking off the set, but then I noticed that Tom Steele hadn't gotten up. Just as I reached him, he was beginning to come round. Without meaning to, I had really nailed him. Tom was out for about twenty seconds.

Of course, I got tagged a time or two myself. I remember while filming *Kit Carson* in 1940, I was in a scene struggling with Indians. George Seitz, the director, wanted us to make it look good and real, and while we were struggling, I got hit across the face with a gun. I had a pretty bad nosebleed— and that was just the rehearsal.

Later on, while I was making *El Dorado Pass* (1948), a Durango Kid Western with Charles Starrett, I got hit so hard it loosened a tooth. Starrett threw a right-hand punch at me, and instead of just missing me as he was supposed to, he tagged me right on the jaw. They called the dentist, who put packing on the tooth so that I could finish the day's shooting. Then I went to his office that night, and he pushed the tooth back in and wired it so it would stay put. The next day was the last day of the picture, and they had to shoot the back of my head because my mouth was messed up.

I had a close call on *The Ghost of Zorro*, too. In a scene in chapter 3, a door is dynamited and comes flying toward the camera. We planned the scene carefully to make sure that I was in no danger. But what we didn't realize is that dynamite has a tendency to build up strength over time. The special effects men rigged up the explosion, and we rehearsed the scene over and over, making sure that every-thing was just so. However, through all that rehearsal time, the dynamite was working, so when they finally blew the door, the blast was bigger than anyone expected. A large chunk of the door came whizzing by me, grazing my head—and it just kept going. Another inch or so and my head would have kept right on going with it.

Fans who came to know my voice very well through *The Lone Ranger* are often either confused or amused (or both) by my voice in *The Ghost of Zorro*. Because the studio wanted a clear contrast between my two characters, I recorded all of Ken Mason's dialog, but Zorro's voice was dubbed by someone else. I didn't know at the time they were doing that—in fact, I only found out when I saw the serial on video a few years ago. I love doing character roles and played everything from an old geezer to the French Father Batiste on *The Lone Ranger*, but I guess the people at Republic didn't know I had that ability. Maybe they just didn't think much of my acting. There is a funny moment, though, in chapter 10. For some reason, they missed dubbing one scene, and you can hear my voice behind Zorro's mask.

I looked at every new job as an opportunity to improve myself and gain some knowledge. On *The Ghost of Zorro*, I learned to do a running mount, which became my favorite. Stuntmen would replace one stirrup with what they called a "step," an L-shaped piece of metal, because stirrups were sometimes a little too narrow to get your boot into when you were leaping like that. I got very good at the running mount, and later on *The Lone Ranger*, I had special wide stirrups made for me, so that I didn't have to use the step.

I also learned the proper way to tie a horse to the hitching post. I saw a lot of Western actors just throw the reins over the rail, but I was taught to make a loop with a tie so that when I came back to remount, I just tugged on the reins and the loop came undone.

Horses can be trained to do a lot of wonderful things. Back in the old days, if a horse needed to fall while running, stunt riders used what they called the "Running W," two wires that attached to the horse's front legs. The rider held the ends of both wires in his fists. When he was supposed to be shot, the rider would fling his arms up, pulling the horse's front legs out from under him. Many horses were injured or killed by this cruel practice, and I'm happy to say that the Running W has now been outlawed. Today horses are trained to fall over to one side, landing safely on their shoulders. The ASPCA now comes to the set to inspect how the animals are being treated and will shut a picture down if animals are being harmed in any way.

But it's difficult to train a horse not to react to gunshots. The loud noise makes them shy, and sometimes they will simply stop in their tracks, or start bucking, terrified. I learned to shoot over a horse's head, not at the side, and to use a quarter-load blank instead of a full load. The prop man always had to know the scene precisely to load your weapon.

Since we used blanks during shoot-outs, the prop men had to invent a way to show a bullet hit. If you were shot in a movie, you were rigged up with a squib, a tiny, safe explosive device that went off and tore a tiny hole in your shirt or wherever you were supposed to be shot. Later on, as movie violence became a little more graphic, tiny bags of blood would be placed over the squib for a more realistic shooting. But I don't believe we ever used body squibs at Republic. We were mindful of not upsetting our young audiences and whatever violence occurred in our Westerns was mild indeed. People were rarely killed in Republic serials—just wounded. And blood was almost never seen.

Squibs *were* used, however, if a bullet was supposed to strike a wall, just missing someone. More often, a prop man would be just offscreen with a pellet gun loaded with capsules filled with fuller's earth. He would fire it at the ground or a rock, and the resulting puff of dust made it look like a bullet had hit there.

Sometimes, watching a serial, you might notice that a character changes clothes suddenly and for no apparent reason. Actually, there's a very *good* reason. It's because the costume has to match up with whatever stock footage that the studio wants to use. There was no problem in *The Ghost of Zorro* because the Zorro costume matched that of all former Zorros and Republic could intercut long shots from any of their previous films. As Ken Mason, I wore a suit that matched one that Red Ryder used in an earlier film. Budgets were always so low on these serials that we looked for any possible way to save a few dollars here and there while still giving the audience maximum entertainment. I believe the low budgets were actually good for us in a way, by forcing us to be even more creative and ingenious about solving problems.

The Ghost of Zorro completed filming in February 1949, and the first episode was released on April 12. I thought that it had turned out well and was proud of what we had accomplished. But there was no reason to think of *The Ghost of Zorro* as anything other than just another serial. I went home to wait for my next assignment from Republic, eager for rest after taking off the Zorro mask.

What I didn't realize is that I wouldn't work for Republic again for a while. And as for masks—I was about to put one on that I would never truly take off again.

CHAPTER SEVEN

Hi Yo Silver! Awayyy!

I was seriously considered for the part of the Lone Ranger before I knew anything about it.

I knew about the character, of course—everybody did. The Lone Ranger and his faithful Indian sidekick Tonto had been righting wrongs on radio since 1933 and in the funny papers since 1938.

The Lone Ranger was the idea of George Washington Trendle. In 1929 Trendle was anxious to develop original programs for radio station WXYZ in Detroit and thought a Western show would be popular. Inspired by the popular character Zorro, Trendle was intrigued by the idea of a mysterious, masked figure of justice. Working with writer Fran Striker and others, Trendle eventually developed this concept, making the masked man a former Texas Ranger. Once that was established, the name came easily—the Lone Ranger.

Another element of the Lone Ranger present from the first radio broadcast on February 2, 1933, was the theme song, Rossini's *William Tell* Overture. Because of *The Lone*

Ranger, this stirring music has become one of the most beloved and recognized classical compositions in history.

Several actors, including John Deeds and George Seaton, played the Lone Ranger on radio in the early years, but the first one who became truly identified with the role was Earle W. Graser. When he died in a car accident in 1941, the part was taken over by Brace Beemer. Beemer is the radio Lone Ranger that I remember most fondly. He had a rich, deep voice that soon became known around the country. Later when I played the character on television, I tried my best to duplicate Beemer's powerful voice and distinctive way of speaking.

In 1938, at the height of the radio show's popularity, Trendle sold the movie rights of *The Lone Ranger* to Republic Pictures. The studio produced an exciting serial that year, starring Lee Powell as the masked man and Chief Thundercloud as Tonto. Chief Thundercloud played the role again a year later in *The Lone Ranger Rides Again*, but this time the Lone Ranger was portrayed by Bob Livingston, one of the popular Three Mesquiteers.

By this time, every kid in America recognized the Lone Ranger's distinctive suit, his white hat, and long black mask. And they knew his strict code of conduct, too: the Lone Ranger always fought for what he believed was right, and he only fired his famous silver bullet to disarm or wound, never to kill.

I was no kid when *The Lone Ranger* began airing on radio station WXYZ in Detroit in 1933; I was already eighteen years old, performing on the trapeze and trampoline with the Flying Behrs. But because I loved Western movies and stories so much, *The Lone Ranger* quickly became a favorite program. It aired three evenings a week in those days, and I tried not to miss an episode. I have warm memories of listening to *The Lone Ranger* with my dad. He loved it; in fact *The Lone Ranger* and *Amos 'n' Andy* were his two favorite radio shows.

So when my agent told me in the spring of 1949 that I was being considered for the leading role in a proposed television version of *The Lone Ranger*, I was thrilled—and more than a little scared.

George W. Trendle, the creator of *The Lone Ranger*, was going to produce the television show, with producer Jack Chertok and writer Fran Striker, the man who first developed the character. That powerful trio began looking for the perfect actor to play the role. An agent, Antrim Short, brought an actor—I don't know who it was—into Chertok's office to meet with Trendle and Striker. They didn't really care for this actor and asked the agent if he had someone else who might be appropriate for the part.

Short told Trendle and Striker, "As far as I'm concerned, there's only one man to play the Lone Ranger, and I'm not his agent."

"Well, who is he?" Trendle asked.

"Clayton Moore," Short said. "He's made several pictures over at Republic. You should take a look at a serial he did a while back, called *Ghost of Zorro*. He's the perfect choice to play the Lone Ranger."

It's interesting that Trendle, who was inspired by the character of Zorro to create the Lone Ranger, was going to check out *my* performance as Zorro to see whether I would be right to play the Lone Ranger. Antrim Short must have liked the way I conveyed character, even through a large black mask—one that covered my face far more than the Lone Ranger's mask would.

Trendle, Chertok, and Striker had a print of *Ghost of Zorro* sent over from Republic, and they watched it. Apparently they thought Short was right because they contacted my agent, Lou Sherrill, and asked him to bring me in immediately.

When we arrived for the appointment with Trendle, Striker, and Chertok, my knees were shaking; I hoped my agent would stick close to me. That hope was dashed immediately. Mr. Trendle asked Lou to sit out in the anteroom and invited me to come in and sit down—alone. There I was with Jack Chertok, George Trendle, and Fran Striker. I didn't realize it then, of course, but my entire future was in their hands.

I knew of Chertok because I had been under contract at MGM where Chertok produced short subjects. I was aware of his reputation as an excellent producer. I had never worked for him, although I knew people who had, including my close friend Tom Neal. With Trendle and Striker, I didn't know what to expect. I knew that Trendle was worth probably twenty million dollars; his life was an amazing success story, having worked his way up from movie theater usher to become one of the most powerful names in broadcasting.

Facing these three imposing men, I didn't know exactly what to do. Would they want me to perform for them? Should I have prepared a monologue of some kind? I wanted very much to play the Lone Ranger and didn't want to do anything to make them think I was wrong for the part.

But, in fact, the subject of the Lone Ranger barely came up in the long conversation that followed. They asked me about previous movie roles, about my earlier life. They were interested to learn about my experience as an acrobat with the Flying Behrs, feeling that the Lone Ranger would have to not only act heroic but look heroic. My athletic ability would be a definite plus. We talked about so many subjects that I almost began to relax. But not quite. I still felt as though I was being given a thorough interrogation and answered every question carefully.

Every so often Mr. Trendle would throw a look over to Fran Striker. Striker would nod or say, "Looks pretty good," then Trendle would question me more. They gave me the third-degree pretty thoroughly, there's no doubt about that. They had me stand up and walk around, turn, take my suit coat off, put it back on. They looked at me full on and in profile, but they didn't have me read any lines.

I didn't have much sense of time, but I presumed I was there for almost an hour with my agent cooling his heels outside. I went up there to get the part of the Lone Ranger and wanted to make a good impression. I tried to study their faces to see how they were reacting to me, but I was never sure if I was winning them over.

Finally they brought my agent back in. Then Mr. Trendle looked directly into my eyes. "Mr. Moore," he said—he didn't call me Clayton, never got that informal—"would you like the part of the Lone Ranger?"

I stiffened up just a little bit, and my knees stopped quaking. I looked back at him and said, "Mr. Trendle, I *am* the Lone Ranger!"

George Washington Trendle replied, "The job is yours."

He told my agent and me to be in Mr. Chertok's office the next morning. That was it. As I drove home, instead of playing the radio, I was whistling the *William Tell* Overture. I started blasting the car horn pretty good when I got to the corner of Greenbush and Laurel Canyon, and kept banging it until I pulled up into our driveway. Sally ran to the door.

"What is it?" she asked.

"I got it! I got it!" I shouted, feeling like a kid. "I'm the Lone Ranger!"

Sally was almost as thrilled as I was. For an actor, it is always a moment of triumph when you get a part that you really want. But this was even bigger somehow. Maybe it was because the Lone Ranger had been a part of my imagination for so long. And maybe it was because I was stepping into a character that was already a part of America's folklore. But when I got that part, I was not only ecstatic, I was *honored*. I knew instinctively that this was not just another job.

§

I didn't realize it at the time, but there was another reason to be excited. By appearing in this show, I would be a part of history: *The Lone Ranger* was the first Western ever produced for television. The networks were already showing Hopalong Cassidy and other Western heroes, but those programs were edited versions of movies originally shown in theaters.

Of course, the Lone Ranger was only one of the two major roles in the television series. An equally important part was the Ranger's faithful Indian sidekick Tonto. When I returned to Chertok's office the next day, I was introduced to the man who had that role.

He was tall and handsome, looking every bit as regal as the son of a Mohawk chief should. Fran Striker said to me, "This is Jay Silverheels. He's going to be your Tonto."

As we shook hands for the first time, I felt as if I had known Jay Silverheels for a long time. There was—not a bond, exactly—but a friendly feeling of warmth between us, as though we instantly understood each other perfectly. We would remain close friends for the next thirty years. In fact, in all the years we worked together, we never had a cross word.

Although Jay was a full-blooded Mohawk from the Six Nations Indian Reservation in Ontario, Canada, he was born with a most un-Indian-sounding name: Harold J. Smith. Like me, he'd started out as an athlete, then began acting in movies in the midforties, appearing in films like *Captain From Castille* (1946), *Yellow Sky* (1948), and *Key Largo* (1948).

I had worked with him before, but I'd never known him. I was on the same set with him on the Gene Autry movie, *The Cowboy and the Indians* (1949). We were even in some of the same scenes, but I had never met Jay Silverheels and never talked to him.

I didn't meet him, in fact, until he was brought into Jack Chertok's office and we learned that we were to be co-stars. From what I understand, Trendle and Striker never considered anyone else for the part of Tonto but Jay Silverheels.

Once I had been cast as the Lone Ranger, I had to start preparing for the filming. First I had to attend to the horse—after all, where would the Lone Ranger be without Silver? I went to a well-known horseman, Hugh Hooker. He and his family raised and trained horses out in the San Fernando Valley and often provided mounts for the movies.

Hugh had two white horses for me to consider, but we never used the second one; he was not as handy or as good looking. The first horse was the stallion that I used. He was a gentle and good-looking stud. I spent a few weeks out there working with him. Although his name was Silver on the screen, on the set we nicknamed him Liver Lip. You can see in some of the publicity pictures he had a big bottom lip. We made fun of him because the bit he used had a copper roller and he would tongue that copper roller so his lip would hang down. When we went into production, we finally had to tape the copper roller down because the sound department was picking up the clatter as he rolled it against his teeth.

Another matter to consider was my voice. Although today most people recognize me more for my voice than my face, I didn't come to the role with the kind of deep, sonorous voice that fans of the radio show knew. Brace Beemer, who played the Lone Ranger on the radio, had that great voice—and I had to match it. I listened to phonograph records of the radio program over and over, whenever I had any free time, and tried to imitate his special way of saying things. Fran Striker advised me to stand in the corner and talk until my voice would hit and bounce back to me. He also advised me to sing a scale, up and down, to get my voice lower, to sound like Brace. I remember driving to the studio, singing up and down, up and down the scale as low as I could go. All of these exercises struck people as pretty funny. Sally used to laugh at me as I stood in the corner talking in a deep, booming voice: "Hello! How are you! Hello!" And singing the scale, "Ah ah ah ah ah ah!" Over and over and over.

But no matter how ridiculous it seemed, it worked. This is how I got the depth that George Trendle wanted. You can hear it. There's a big difference between the tone of my voice in *The Perils of Nyoka* in 1942 and *The Lone Ranger* in 1949. That difference came about through practicing and singing and talking in the corner like a little boy being punished.

My first costume was made by Frank Acuna, an independent costumer. It was very similar to the standard Lone

Ranger costume, except that the first mask was slightly smaller and covered less of my face. The mask was made of plaster, molded right to my face, then covered with purple felt. I developed the molded mask. In previous movies, masked men had trouble moving around because the mask hindered their vision. But with this mask, I had no trouble at all. I could see a punch coming from the side, or I could look down and see my toes.

The first mask was also purple, not black. Because we were shooting the first episodes of *The Lone Ranger* in black and white, the purple color delivered a more textured look, not such a dead black. Our costumes came in slightly different colors, depending on whether we were shooting indoors or on location, so that the colors would look right on black-and-white film.

With so much of my face covered by the mask, it was especially important for my eyes to register effectively. They used a little magenta light, called a "hinky dink," that was set right next to the camera and directed specifically at my eyes. In close-ups, the hinky dink helped to bring my eyes out. It sounds painful, but I don't recall it as a problem.

What *was* painful was the mask itself. Well, not painful exactly, but uncomfortable. It got pretty hot on location. Sometimes the sweat would just pour out. The costume got pretty warm, too, but that's a problem all actors must face. It's rare that something that looks good on screen is also light and comfortable to wear.

Our cameraman was Mack Stengler, who had been photographing movies since the early twenties. Mack was an exact cameraman. If your mark was here, you hit that mark, but without looking down.

We really needed a professional cameraman and crew

because of the speed at which we worked. Believe it or not, we filmed those first episodes of *The Lone Ranger* in about two days each. That's almost *fifteen minutes* of completed footage every day. You probably couldn't find television performers today who *could* work that fast, even if they were willing.

We began production on the series on June 21, 1949. Even by the standards of the day, our budgets were low. For the first two seasons, *The Lone Ranger* cost $12,500 per episode. Our sponsor General Mills raised the budget to $15,000 in 1951, $17,000 in 1952, and $18,000 by 1954. Today it isn't unusual for a four-minute music video on MTV to cost a million dollars. We were really masters at stretching a buck back then.

One of the ways we kept to our budgets was to plan each episode's production carefully. Our routine was to shoot the location scenes first, then move into the studio for interior scenes. We kept a quick pace. We sometimes shot three episodes in a week. After six or eight episodes in a row, then we'd lay off for a few weeks to give the writers time to come up with new scripts.

The first episode, of course, introduced the Lone Ranger and Tonto and showed how the Long Ranger came to wear the mask and how he found Silver. The character's real name is Reid (he was never actually given a first name, although somehow people have come to believe his first name was John). Reid is one of six Texas Rangers, including his older brother Dan, in pursuit of a gang headed up by the evil Butch Cavendish. The rangers are led into an ambush where they are all killed by Cavendish's men—all, that is, except one. This wounded ranger is discovered by an Indian, Tonto, who nurses him back to health. They had met as boys, when Tonto had nicknamed him Kimo Sabe, which meant trusty scout.

The Lone Ranger vows to bring Cavendish to justice but knows that he can do the job better if no one knows who he is. The world thinks that he died along with the other six rangers, and so he decides to let the world continue to believe that he is dead. Tonto suggests that he should wear a mask to keep from being recognized. He makes the mask from the vest of his dead brother. After he finds and tames a beautiful white stallion in Wild Horse Canyon, the Lone Ranger and Tonto are ready to ride, bringing justice to the West.

That first episode aired on September 15, 1949, the day after my thirty-fifth birthday. Sally and I had been invited to some friends' home to celebrate. Just as the program was about to start, their television starting acting up. Our friend started working on it with a screwdriver—and after that the television didn't work at all. That didn't bother me as much as it did everyone else. After all, I didn't *need* to see it—I already knew how the episode turned out. Besides, I was far more interested in making the programs than in watching them.

The locations for several *Lone Ranger* episodes were shot at one time. Before we shot a picture, the location manager, the assistant director, and the director would go out and canvas the area. It was rough country, but you could take your camera truck and your sound truck up to all these wild spots. Nearly all the exteriors, particularly in the first season of *The Lone Ranger*, were filmed at Iverson's Ranch in Chatsworth. This rugged location had been the backdrop of hundreds of great Westerns from the silent days right up to the present. At the summit of one of Iverson's hills is a unique grouping of large rocks known as

Garden of the Gods. Those rocks concealed many a bad guy, waiting to rob the stagecoach or ambush the sheriff. The ambush sequence in our first episode, however, was shot in Bronson Canyon in Hollywood.

As a money-saving device, Trendle and Chertok used some of the same action sequences in several different episodes. If they went to the expense to stage a runaway stagecoach or other such elaborate scene, viewers could count on seeing it in three or four episodes over the course of the season. But cost cutting aside, Iverson's Ranch was a place of such beauty and drama that it made even low-budget television shows as ours look spectacular.

On one occasion we traveled to Apple Valley in the high desert above Los Angeles for two weeks to shoot some stock footage. No sound, whatsoever. We took a truck full of horses, wagons, and doubles, as well as costume changes for other characters, male and female, but no actors except Jay and myself. Jay and I used to get a kick out of seeing the stuntmen sporting pioneer dresses—and beards. We filmed stock shots: the doubles in chases, runs, fights, riding buckboards and covered wagons. We ran a stagecoach along a dirt road and chased bad guys. The footage we shot in those two weeks showed up in episodes for seasons to come.

You may have noticed that during fight scenes the Lone Ranger's hat never came off. That's because of a little trick I learned from stuntman Tom Steele. I took a rubber tube, the kind you would use as a tourniquet—it was about as thick as your little finger—and put that on the inside of the hat band. Then, when I put the hat on and pushed it on, it made the hat tight so it wouldn't come off. Sometimes, if it wouldn't show up on screen, I would use the chin strap, too.

Fight scenes were always shot in sections. The stuntmen blocked it out so they would always know the perfect spot for the close-up of me or Tonto or whoever. I would usually get two or three good close-ups in a fight scene. When I did serials at Republic, it was a little different because serial fights were usually much longer than *The Lone Ranger* fight routines.

Bill Ward usually doubled me for those action scenes. Although both Jay and I were athletic, we generally used stunt doubles. At the pace we were shooting, it made the front office nervous if we performed our own stunts. We did two or three episodes a week, and if I got hurt, they would have had to shut down the whole production. So I used to take each stunt as it came. If I thought I could do it, I'd do it. If I didn't, they used Bill, Al Wyatt, or Alan Pinson.

But remember the opening scene, in front of Lone Ranger Rock, where Silver rears up? That's me. I did all the rearing of the horse. Not because I thought I was such an excellent horseman that no one else could rear Silver as well as I could, but because every time they used that shot to advertise the show, I got fifty dollars. So I made sure that every time we reared that horse, I was on him.

The interiors for *The Lone Ranger* were filmed down in Culver City at the old Hal Roach Studios, where the *Our Gang* and Laurel and Hardy shorts were filmed in the twenties and thirties. There was a Western street there, as well as a sheriff's office and a farmhouse. There was even a "green set" that tried its hardest to resemble an outdoor location with bushes, trees, and other greenery. I don't think this phony-looking set ever fooled anybody, even the less sophisticated television viewers of the fifties. But nobody complained—it was all in the spirit of fun.

Through it all, to make sure that I maintained that

deep Lone Ranger voice, I used to cup my hand over my ear before every scene and repeat lines of dialog. The assistant director and the crew used to break up watching me stand there saying to myself, "Dan Reid. I want you to know, Dan...."

I always needed a few moments to myself before doing a scene. I would go into a corner or into my dressing room and quiet down for about ten or twenty seconds, just to relax and concentrate. We were shooting at such a fast rate that I needed this time to help me remember my lines and everything else that scenes required. We had no teleprompters to help us remember our dialogue, and I used to blow my lines pretty good. But we always had at least one rehearsal before we filmed the scene, just to block it out.

The Lone Ranger was not the only show filming on the Roach lot, and sometimes, between setups, we would wander over to another set to watch other companies at work. One day my stunt double Bill Ward went to watch a high school picture being filmed nearby. He was gone for about an hour, and when he returned, he had a kind of awestruck look on his face.

"Hey," Bill said, "I want you and Jay to come over and see a girl who is working on the next stage."

We wandered over to the set, and Bill pointed her out. "See that young girl over there?" Bill said. She was a stunning blonde with a spectacular figure. Even though she was doing just a bit part, you could see immediately that she had something special. Bill said, "She's the most beautiful thing I've ever seen."

It was Marilyn Monroe.

Bill finally introduced himself to her and brought her over to our set, and the crew was just stymied, she was that attractive. In those days the girls wore long dresses and bobby socks and saddle shoes. Marilyn, however, would have knocked you out if she had been wearing only a canvas sack; she was a striking young girl.

But I was married, and Jay and I were wrapped up in our work. So we threw another long look at her, but that was about it.

Working so fast didn't give us a great deal of time to work on our performances. We only rehearsed until we got the dialogue down, then we learned where our marks were, made sure we were in the proper key light, which came from up above, and off we went.

When I watch those early episodes today, they evoke amateur night. Mr. Trendle had me talk slowly, very pedantically. He would press me to "make sure you pronounce each word clearly." He required perfect diction, and I was continually told to "talk slowly." We were never allowed to change the dialogue that Mr. Trendle had okayed.

Of course, we weren't machines. Every now and then something went wrong. Mr. Trendle didn't come to the set much. Instead, Fred Froelich, his "cover man," would drop in on us occasionally. If anything went wrong, you went to Fred Froelich first, and then he carried it to George W. Trendle.

On one episode, directed by George Seitz Jr., whose father had directed *Kit Carson*, Jay and I had a two-shot—a scene with two actors, shot in one long take—about two pages long.

Fred Froelich sat near George and the script girl. We went through the first page without a hitch and came down to the second page. At about the second paragraph before the end of the scene, I had to say to Tonto, "It was just a trick that Trigger Taylor tried to pull."

That's a real tongue twister. It was a tough scene, done with no individual shots to break it up. We went for the first take, and when we got down to the second page and came to that line, I blew it.

We went for the second take. I blew it again. I think I blew it five or six times. We'd get the first page fine, get to the top of the second page—so far, so good—then come down to that one line, and I'd mess it up every time.

Finally I said to the director, "George, that's a tough line. Can we change it?"

George looked at Fred Froelich, who said to read it just as George Trendle had okayed the line: "It was just a trick that Trigger Taylor tried to pull."

I pleaded with George, "Let's change the line."

Froelich said, "You read it exactly the way Trendle has it, Clay."

So we tried it again. Meanwhile the crew was betting that I'd blow it. When I came to "that Trigger Taylor tried to pull," I muffed it.

I looked at the director, then looked down at Fred Froelich and said, "Fred, will you leave the set?"

He looked at George, looked hard at me, then he got up and walked away, saying, "Mr. Trendle will hear about this."

They loaded the camera and prepared for the next take. There was the first page. Then came the second page. When I got to that line I said, "You know, Tonto, it was just a trick that Taylor tried to pull."

Jay said, "Ah, that right, Kimo Sabe."

I said, "Let's go!"

The crew applauded and collected their bets. Of course, I heard about it from Mr. Trendle. But what can you do?

Jay's dialogue was treated the same way. Often he was

the only Indian in the script to speak with broken English. It might have been embarrassing for him, but he never said anything about it; he knew he was playing a part.

In one episode Jay had a tongue twister of his own. We rode into the scene, dismounted, ran up a short hill, crouched down at a fallen log, and Jay said, "Kimo Sabe, me see snoke sniggle."

Well, I started to laugh. Jay did, too. But it meant we had to go down the hill, mount the horses, and do the whole scene again.

Unfortunately on the second take, Jay said "snoke sniggle" again. This time we collapsed in laughter. By the fourth take, the horses were blowing pretty hard, but we could barely stop laughing. On the fifth take Jay finally got it: "Kimo Sabe, me see smoke signal."

We heard the director say, "Print it!" And under his breath, "It's about time!"

One episode on the set with Jay wasn't so funny, however. Although Jay was a great athlete, he was a heavy smoker (as I was in those days). In one scene, Jay was doing a fight with a stuntman who, at one point, fell on top of Jay. I was sitting there watching them do the fight, and when Jay walked to his dressing room, I noticed he walked kind of funny. I went over to the makeup table where Gene Hibbs (who was also Ann Sothern's makeup man) was sitting.

I said, "Was Jay walking all right when he went by you?"

"No," Gene replied, "he wasn't his usual self."

I went into Jay's dressing room, and he was sitting there, hunched over, holding his chest. They sent him to the infirmary, then drove him in a limo to the hospital. He'd had a heart attack.

We had to shut down production while the writers

came up with new scripts to explain Tonto's absence. During this break in filming, Sally and I went to Minneapolis to visit her family. I got a phone call one night telling me to hurry back to Hollywood—we were going back into production. They had finally decided to say that Tonto was visiting Washington, D.C., "seeing the Great White Father."

They had also decided to introduce the character of Dan Reid, the Lone Ranger's nephew, while Jay was out. (Dan's father was killed in the Texas Ranger ambush in the first episode.) Dan was played by Chuck Courtney, who was a good friend and an excellent actor. The character, introduced in episode twenty-two and featured in six or eight shows, acted as the Lone Ranger's sidekick.

I remember several other actors who appeared in *Lone Ranger* episodes around that time: DeForest Kelly, who later played Dr. McCoy on *Star Trek*, Harry Lauder, Denver Pyle, Marjorie Lord, Jack Elam, many other fine performers. Dennis Weaver did a bit in *The Lone Ranger* before he found fame on *Gunsmoke*, and Marion Ross, later a star of *Happy Days*, also worked with us. Jim Arness, too, when he was just starting out. In those days I believe the actors were paid forty-five dollars a day.

Jay only missed a few shows, and we kept a pretty close eye on him when he returned. He always carried nitroglycerin tablets. From then on, his action in the series was not so strenuous.

We did seventy-nine episodes of *The Lone Ranger* with Jack Chertok. Audiences embraced the show right away, keeping it in the top fifteen rated programs in those years. Jay and I would support the show by making personal appearances around the country. I was always impressed by the respect the children had for the Lone Ranger costume and mask. Other stars complain of being manhandled by crowds, but that never happened to us.

Once, though, I was in the middle of a crowd when I noticed tugging on my belt. I turned and saw a couple of kids trying to push the bullets out of the holster in the back.

I knelt down and looked them right in the eye. "You know, boys," I said, "these silver bullets are the symbol of justice, fair play, and honesty." I peered closer at them. "Tonto and I fight for law and order. When someone takes something he's not supposed to, it disappoints us, because it makes us feel like we're on opposite sides."

The boys looked stricken. I said, "Don't you want to help Tonto and the Lone Ranger uphold the law?" The look on their faces was something to see. They both nodded.

I stood up. "I know you do," I said. "You're good boys." I shook them both by the hand and then turned back to the crowd. Jay and I always stressed fair play and honesty. It was what the characters demanded, but it was also what we personally believed.

These good ideals were all a part of *The Lone Ranger*, but there was nothing preachy about the shows. They were fast paced, entertaining, and could be enjoyed by people of all ages. But I believe their enduring popularity stems from the character of the Lone Ranger himself.

Fran Striker once told me, "When we dreamed up the character of the Lone Ranger, George Trendle said to me, 'I don't want a superman. I want a real, authentic, true-to-life hero.'" I think audiences sensed that the Lone Ranger, although brave and resourceful, was only human and could be placed in real danger. An audience roots harder for a vulnerable man than for some superhero with supernatural strength. In fact, back when the Lone Ranger was new, Striker wrote "The Lone Ranger Creed," an inspiring passage that summed up what the character was all about. I always keep a copy of it with me.

The Lone Ranger Creed

I believe that to have a friend, a man must be one. That all men are created equal and that everyone has within himself the power to make this a better world. That God put the firewood there but that every man must gather and light it himself. In being prepared physically, mentally and morally to fight when necessary for that which is right. That a man should make the most of what equipment he has. That 'This government, of the people, by the people and for the people' shall live always. That men should live by the rule of what is best for the greatest number. That sooner or later. . . somewhere. . . somehow. . . we must settle with the world and make payment for what we have taken. That all things change but truth, and that truth alone, lives on forever. In my Creator, my country, my fellow man.

THE LONE RANGER

That creed pretty much summed up my own convictions, too. I believed in the show and in the character and in all the things they stood for. I was awfully proud to be the Lone Ranger.

That's why it came as such a shock to me when—without warning or explanation—George Trendle fired me. One day I was doing a job I loved, idolized by children all across the country. The next, I was out of a job.

And I didn't know why.

CHAPTER EIGHT

Back to the Big Screen

No one connected with *The Lone Ranger* ever told me why I had been fired—and I never asked. That may seem strange, but I wasn't the sort of person to go in and make a scene about something like that. Such things happened in show business all the time. You got a part or lost a part, sometimes just on the whim of a producer or because the show was taking a new turn.

Of course, I've heard many rumors over the years. The most prominent one was that I demanded more money and when I didn't receive it, I quit. That isn't true. I've also heard that George Trendle got the idea that I wanted to horn in on *The Lone Ranger*'s merchandising. He never asked me about it. If he had, I would have told him it wasn't the case. I was never interested in that kind of thing, although I probably should have been. *Lone Ranger* toys, games, clothes, and memorabilia were produced over the years and made millions for somebody—but not me.

John Hart replaced me on *The Lone Ranger*. John had appeared in several episodes with me, usually playing a heavy. I thought he was a great guy and a fine actor and was glad to see the part go to someone I knew would do a first-rate job. Jay Silverheels stayed on as Tonto, and we continued to be close friends.

All in all, losing the part of the Lone Ranger didn't affect me nearly as much as it would have if it had happened a few years later. The character became more and more important to me over time, but at this point, I was able to let it go.

After all, I had no choice. I was out of work, and all I could do was get back in the swim again. Actually I was intrigued by what my next part would be. No matter how much I had enjoyed playing the Lone Ranger, playing a different character would be a refreshing change.

My first role was about as different from the Lone Ranger as you can imagine. Republic Pictures wanted me back to play a heavy in a new science fiction serial *Radar Men from the Moon* (1952), featuring their popular character Commando Cody. (I was never under contract at Republic, by the way; I was just hired as a freelance actor, from picture to picture.)

I relished the chance to sink my teeth into a real bad-guy role again. Heavies were fun because you could play strong emotions and let loose. Heroes were usually tight-lipped and stern. Villains were colorful and sometimes campy. I was reunited with director Fred Brannon on *Radar Men from the Moon*, and the cast included such old pals as Roy Barcroft, Tom Steele, and Dale Van Sickel. George Wallace played Commando Cody and Aline Towne played the heroine, Joan Gilbert. By the way, my buddy Tris Coffin played Commando Cody in other serials.

The plot is one of those whimsical, farfetched stories only acceptable in a serial. Retik, an evil ruler on the Moon, is trying to conquer the Earth with an atomic ray. When Commando

Cody gets wind of this, he flies to the Moon with Joan and his assistant Ted and battles Retik in his huge laboratory. Something earth (or rather, moon) shattering happened in every episode—ray-gun attacks, a volcanic eruption—along with plenty of fights, chases, and cliffhangers.

The Moon, of course, was actually Iverson's Ranch. We also filmed at the Republic Cave and in Topanga Canyon. Just as in the old days, Tom Steele doubled me, although I did one stunt myself. In chapter 3 my character was supposed to jump out of a car and roll down the hill. It didn't seem like such a hard stunt to me, so I did it before anyone could tell me no. Luckily, everything went fine. I wasn't making much money and wasn't on the show for long. So I guess they figured even if something did happen to me, it was no great loss.

George Wallace and I had a fight scene in *Radar Men*. As always, we thought it through thoroughly. I was supposed to hit him with my right hand, but because I was coming at him from an angle, my head would be turned and I wouldn't see him. It was up to him to dodge the punch, so the camera would make it appear as if I had hit him. I said, "I'll swing at you, and as I'm coming around, you throw a punch at me and I'll block it with my left hand. Now remember, I can't see you, so be out of the way."

George said, "Don't worry, I've done a lot of stage work. I can take your punch. I'll be right there for you."

We started the fight scene, and when we got to that point, I swung and he didn't move. I cracked him right on the nose. The bad part was that he'd had his nose operated on not long before that. It must have been incredibly painful, but he didn't say a word about it. They had to pack his face in ice. I felt terrible about it, but those things sometimes happen.

Even though I had been gone for about three years, things hadn't changed much at Republic. Directors still had to scrape every bit of footage together for the lowest possible budget. Freddy Brannon padded *Radar Men from the Moon* with footage from *King of the Rocket Men* (1949), *Darkest Africa* (1936), and *The Purple Monster Strikes* (1945).

But there were also some fine special effects used in films like these. The Lydecker brothers, Howard and Theodore, directed special effects and worked some impressive magic with tiny budgets. For instance, to make Commando Cody fly, the Lydeckers would put him on a wire and let him glide to earth feet first. When they reversed the film, he took off like—well, like Commando Cody.

Son of Geronimo (1952) was more down to earth—literally. It was a solid, fast-paced Western directed by one of the best serial directors of them all, Spencer Gordon Bennet. Bennett had been around for years, directing his first serial, *The Black Book*, in 1929. In fact, he directed the very last movie serial ever made, *Blazing the Overland Trail* (1956). He knew his stuff.

I read over the *Son of Geronimo* script and decided I could handle all the stunts myself. It was one of the few pictures in which I used no stunt doubles at all. I'm sure if there had been something dangerous, they would have brought in Tom Steele or Dave Sharpe. But I remember hearing the cameraman tell Spence, "Don't worry about Clay, he'll do all his own horse work."

We shot *Son of Geronimo* at Pioneer Town, about thirty miles north of Palm Springs. A simple set was there, one used often in the fifties, especially for television Westerns. Russell Hayden, a great sidekick in the Hopalong Cassidy films, had built his own Western town there, too, just across the way. It was used mostly for Edgar Buchanan's television series *Judge Roy Bean*, but we shot there as well.

Speaking of sidekicks, we had a great one in *Son of Geronimo*: Bud Osborn. He had actually been a cowboy on a working ranch when he was younger and was a stagecoach expert. He could drive with teams of four or six horses. I guess Bud was in his sixties by this time. I remember he told me, "I'm going to put a lot of character into this part."

I said, "What do you mean?"

"Well," he drawled, "I'm thinking about chewing tobacco." That was his idea of adding character. Of course when you see him in the film—chewing and spitting—you know that he was right. He was a real character.

Making serials sure didn't get any easier over the years. We always worked longer than an eight-hour day. I usually didn't get home until eight-thirty or nine at night. I'd call Sally from the studio and tell her, "I'm coming home." I wanted her to know so she'd meet me at the door with a little toddy.

We had to be in makeup at 7 A.M. Sally told me that many times she would wake up and I'd be lying there beside her with a script in my hand, sound asleep.

During this period, I was billing myself as "Clay Moore" instead of "Clayton Moore." In retrospect, I realize what a mistake that was. I should have made sure the *Lone Ranger* fans knew where to find me in other pictures, but for some reason or other I wanted to separate myself from the show. I have no idea why.

What I *should* have separated myself from was my next serial. *Jungle Drums of Africa* (1953) was, without a doubt, the worst production I ever appeared in. In fact, it's probably one of the worst serials ever made. Serials weren't noted for brilliant scripts and glossy production values anyway, but even by the standards of the form, *Jungle Drums of Africa* was a real loser. We always tried to infuse tempo into the serials. The action and situations were farfetched, but if you kept the story moving, audiences would enjoy the action without questioning the logic too much. And that was *Jungle Drums of Africa*'s main failing—it just had no tempo.

Also, by this time, serials were no longer the draw they had been. Television was making a serious dent in the movie-going audience. Before television, kids couldn't wait for Saturdays so they could catch the next episode of a thrilling cliffhanger. But television series were offering the same kinds of situations—for free.

After having been the Moon in a previous serial, Iverson's Ranch now stood in for darkest Africa. The prop men didn't change the landscape too much. They just brought in some potted trees and bushes that could be carried around from location to location. I think we crouched behind the same four bushes in various places throughout the entire serial.

My co-star was Phyllis Coates, famous with television fans for being one of the two actresses who played Lois Lane opposite George Reeves in *Superman*. We both knew how silly *Jungle Drums* was, and we frequently broke up at the ridiculous situations. The special effects consisted of prop men just out of camera range throwing fuller's earth and arrows and spears at us. In one scene Phyllis was supposed to be sucked through a wind tunnel. They just tied a rope around her ankles and pulled her through. Now *that's* special effects.

I had a fight scene in a trading post with Henry Rowland. We rehearsed it a couple of times, but I guess we should have rehearsed a little longer. There were some shovels hanging on the wall. Henry grabbed one and we struggled over it. I was supposed to knock it out of his hand, but Henry accidentally brought it down hard, and the point clipped the top of my head. Henry felt terrible about it and went with me to first aid. It really hurt, and bled a little, but the show must go on. The wound was cleaned and dressed, and I was back on the set minutes later.

By the way, most fight scenes or action scenes in serials were "undercranked." This meant that the camera was run at a slightly slower speed so when the scene was projected at normal speed, everything would move just a little faster. We tried not to make it look unnatural—we just wanted a little more zing to the scene. Of course, when undercranking wasn't done right, the actors zipped around the screen like a Keystone Kops movie, creating an absurd scene. If you watch enough serials of the era, you'll see undercranking done both well and badly. It all depended on who was in charge and how well he knew his stuff.

Because of the African setting, there were several African-American actors and extras on the set of *Jungle Drums of Africa*. I've often been asked, because this took place in the pre–Civil Rights era, if any racial tensions or prejudices were present on the set. I honestly don't remember any. A universal bond of camaraderie among actors transcended even the prevailing attitudes of the fifties. Everyone was pleasant and cooperative. There were no prima donnas; everyone had to work together because we had a lot of pages to get through and it was hard, demanding work.

I also appeared around this same time in a feature film that didn't have much more to recommend it than *Jungle Drums of Africa* did. It was called *Buffalo Bill in Tomahawk Territory* (1952), released through United Artists. I played

Buffalo Bill trying to end an Indian uprising. There are bad men who want to keep the warfare going to drive the Indians off their land, which is rich with gold.

The budget for *Buffalo Bill in Tomahawk Territory* made Republic's budgets seem astronomical. Even though the film was barely an hour long, it was padded with stock footage and was low on action or interest.

My next serial, *Gunfighters of the Northwest* (1953), was both more enjoyable to make and more satisfying to watch. It was directed by the master, Spencer Gordon Bennet, and had all the pace, tempo, and excitement that *Jungle Drums* lacked.

Gunfighters of the Northwest was the only picture I ever appeared in that was shot *entirely* outside. There wasn't a single interior scene. Even in a scene where we're supposed to be in a cave, Spence set up the lighting with a backdrop to make it appear that we were inside when in fact it was an exterior shot.

We filmed at beautiful Big Bear, a mountain resort northeast of Los Angeles. Fairly remote at that time, it had been used in such classic pictures as *The Trail of the Lonesome Pine* (1936) and *Brigham Young, Frontiersman* (1940). It took about a month to film the serial, and the whole cast and crew lived in a rustic hotel there. Everyone became close, like a family.

One of my co-stars in *Gunfighters of the Northwest* was Jock Mahoney. Jock and I had been friends for years. Earlier in our careers, Jock was the stunt double for Charlie Starrett in *El Dorado Pass* (1948), one of the Durango Kid Westerns that I appeared in, directed by Ray Nazarro. Jock and I had a fight scene in a mine for that movie. An old ore car was there, and we figured out how to make use of it. We started fighting, and Jock (doubling for Starrett) hit me with an upper cut. I did a flip and landed in the ore cart. Jock went over to Ray Nazarro and said, "Hey, this young fellow did a good fight. Who is he?"

Ray told him I was an ex-trapeze performer and that piqued Jock's interest.

"Clay," Jock said, "I hear you used to work on the trapeze."

"That's right," I said. "I used to be in an act called the Flying Behrs in Chicago. There were five of us."

Jock said, "You know, I used to do a little trapeze work myself at University of Iowa."

"That's a coincidence," I said. "One of our guys went to Iowa University—Bob Vin."

"Bob Vin!?" Jock cried. "I *know* Bob Vin! I used to work on the trapeze rigging that he set up at Iowa U. He had it mounted over the pool because we didn't have a net."

Of course, that was the very rigging that we had built in Johnny Behr's yard years earlier, the one we had used at the 1934 Chicago World's Fair. And here I was in Hollywood working with somebody who had actually used *my* trapeze. Small world, huh?

I went on to work with Jock several times and always enjoyed it. He was always clowning—what a great sense of humor. He was a great athlete, too, legs of rubber. We were on television series at roughly the same time. He starred in *The Range Rider* (1951-52) and *Yancey Derringer* (1958-59). Sally and I lived in Tarzana at the time of *Gunfighters of the Northwest*, and Jock and Jay Silverheels were frequent guests. What grand guys they were, and how much I miss both of them.

I rode a beautiful quarter horse in this serial—fifteen

hands high and extremely intelligent. I tried to buy her, but her owners wouldn't sell. I even thought she was a beauty after she almost killed me.

On about the second day of shooting, Spence wanted to get a shot of me riding straight at the camera, then peeling off to the right at the last minute. We were galloping along when the horse saw a white surveyor's stake. She jumped. As soon as she did, I pushed out of the stirrups because I knew I was going to be in trouble. The horse bucked. I flew straight up in the air, came down flat on my back, and was out like a light. Jock told me later that he said, "Give Clayton a beer and he'll be all right."

The assistant director took me to the doctor in Big Bear. The doctor said I was going to be laid up for a little while. I asked the doctor if there was a chiropractor in town, and he said there was one down the street. I limped, nearly doubled over, into the chiropractor's office. I could hardly move. After he worked me over, I walked out standing straight up. I never did get the beer that Jock mentioned, however.

Later that day Jock Mahoney was doing a fight scene and wrecked the metatarsal in his foot. So we were both laid up. He was walking fine the next day, and when I asked him how he healed so fast, he answered, "Metaphysics."

Now, here's a plot twist as interesting as anything the serial writers ever came up with. Phyllis Coates was once again my co-star. At that time Phyllis was seeing John Hart, the man who had replaced me as the Lone Ranger. John happened to be visiting Phyllis on the set when I hurt myself. When they needed someone to double me in a riding scene, he volunteered. He actually ended up doubling me in several scenes. I could perform all of my dramatic scenes, but it was still several days before I could mount a horse again.

I don't think the irony of the situation escaped either of us. One Lone Ranger doubling another—if that isn't an odd turn of events, I don't know what is.

It got even stranger. By the time the first episode of *Gunfighters of the Northwest* premiered on March 18, 1953, John Hart had already filmed his last *Lone Ranger* episode. I was contacted by George W. Trendle's office a few months later and told that they wanted me to come back to the show.

My serial days were behind me, and the most rewarding part of my career was coming up.

CHAPTER NINE

Jay Silverheels

Through all the years I portrayed the Lone Ranger in movies and on television, I worked with many people. The show had several directors and producers, dozens of writers, hundreds of actors, and who knows how many crew members. I even worked with two different Silvers.

There was only one constant over the entire period— Jay Silverheels.

In the beginning we were just a couple of actors playing in a series together. But as the years went by, we became the best of friends. In the original *Lone Ranger* radio show in the thirties and forties, Tonto was treated as a servant. But in the television scripts, Jay and I played equals. I stressed our equality and brotherhood whenever I could. Although it was not written into any scripts, whenever Jay left to go into town I would say, "Be careful, Tonto." That ad-libbed line was my way of showing how much I cared for him and admired him.

Jay was a full-blooded Mohawk, born on May 26, 1919, on the Six Nations Indian Reservation, Brantford, Ontario, Canada. He was one of seven brothers and sisters. His real name, Harold J. Smith, wasn't legally changed to Jay Silverheels until 1971. Jay and I had a great deal in common, not least of which was the fact that we both started out as athletes before we turned to acting. Whereas I had been a trapeze artist, Jay had pursued a promising career as a wrestler, boxer, and lacrosse player. He won two wrestling championships, finished second in the Eastern Square finals of the Golden Gloves boxing championship in Madison Square Garden, and became a very successful member of Canada's National Lacrosse Team. It was with this team that Jay came to the United States in 1938.

He never told me how he caught the acting bug—I read somewhere that comedian Joe E. Brown encouraged him to get into movies—but he was so handsome, with such a powerful voice, I'm not surprised that he was discovered by filmmakers. Jay appeared in supporting roles in movies like *Too Many Girls* (1940) and *Valley of the Sun* (1942). In some of these early films, he was billed as Silverheels Smith.

Even after we began co-starring in *The Lone Ranger*, Jay continued to appear in features. He was particularly proud of having portrayed the great Indian chief Geronimo in two different films: *Broken Arrow* (1950) and *Walk the Proud Land* (1956).

A most interesting thing happened to me, thanks to our friendship. I was initiated into the Six Nations as a blood brother. During a big gathering on their reservation near Syracuse, New York, they put the beaded and scroffed armband on me. I sat with the Chief and then entered, with the tribe, into the ceremonial dance, after which I was declared a blood brother.

I was moved and impressed at being so accepted by these men. After all, as Jay often reminded me, his ancestors had been on hand to welcome mine when they arrived in America from England on the *Good Ship Anne* way back in 1623.

Jay was dedicated to helping other Native American actors. He was strongly opposed to the practice of hiring white actors to play Indians. He thought it was important to give Native American actors the opportunity to play those roles themselves. The films would be more authentic, and the roles would also help give his people a sense of pride about themselves and their contributions to this country. Jay put his money where his mouth was. In the late 1960s he formed the Indian Actors Workshop in Echo Park and actively encouraged talented young performers to study their craft there.

We worked together almost seamlessly on *The Lone Ranger* programs. Although our roles were usually serious, behind the scenes we always cracked jokes and tried to make each other laugh. Here's one example: Although Jay, of course, was intelligent and articulate, Tonto, the character, was not altogether comfortable with the English language. Jay often broke up at the things Tonto had to say; the phrase "Me do!" turned into kind of a running gag between us. He would say, "Are you going to lunch with us, Clay?" and I would reply, "Yeah, me do!" Or I would be studying my dialogue at about 7:45 in the morning because we were on the set at 8:00. Jay would come in about fifteen minutes before he put his costume on and say, "What are we going to do today, Clay?" I would tell him the title of that episode and he would ask, "What do I say?"

I'd say, "Oh, just say your usual."

"Oh yeah," Jay would grunt before walking away. "Me do."

Despite his sparse dialogue, Jay was a superior actor. He spoke pedantically at times because it was necessary for the character. He never used the short form or slang. His phrasing was excellent. Even when he was given one or two pages of dialogue, he almost never needed more than one take. I can only remember rare instances when Jay ever blew a line, like the "Me see snoke sniggle" incident. More important, perhaps, he had a magnetic presence on the screen. When I watch *Lone Ranger* episodes, my eyes are always on Jay, never on me. He really had a command of his craft. There's a phrase in our business, "He has a face that the camera loves." That was certainly true of Jay Silverheels. I admired his talent a great deal.

I also admired his courage and willingness to stand up for a principle. When we filmed on location at Iverson's ranch, we would park our cars at a gas station at Devonshire, then board a bus that would take us out to the set. There were no dressing rooms for us—we changed clothes in the bus. One day I was putting my costume on and noticed that Jay wasn't getting dressed.

I asked him what was going on, and he replied, "This isn't right. We should have dressing rooms."

It didn't bother me too much that we didn't have dressing rooms. I had gotten my education at Republic Pictures, and that was no-frills movie making. But I could tell it was really getting under Jay's skin. He finally put his costume on, but when we got up to the ranch, he stepped off the bus, mounted his horse Scout, and rode off.

Eight o'clock came and we were ready for the first shot of the day, but Jay was nowhere to be found. Earl Bellamy was directing this episode and after we waited ten or fifteen minutes, Earl asked if I knew where Jay was. I said, "I think I have an idea." I told him that Jay was upset and felt that we weren't being treated fairly.

Earl said, "Every minute we don't shoot is costing us thousands of dollars. Please go find Jay and see what you can do about it."

I told Earl, "I know where he is." I got on Silver and rode up to a large rock where I figured he had gone, a secluded place we often frequented when we wanted to study our lines or spend a few moments resting or concentrating on an upcoming scene. I was right. Jay was there, sitting quietly. I told him we were ready to shoot. Jay said, "I want a dressing room. We're professional actors in a hit series, and I don't think it's right for us to have to change on the bus."

"You may be right, Jay," I said, "but the show must go on."

He got up into Scout's saddle and headed back for the set. He wanted to make sure that his complaint was registered, but he was far too professional to leave his coworkers waiting. We did the scene without a hitch. He would never put his personal feelings ahead of doing his job to the best of his abilities.

But he had delivered his message too. The next morning we had dressing rooms.

During the years following *The Lone Ranger*, Jay and I made a few personal appearances together. But generally we toured separately. Jay had a great show that highlighted Native American culture. The fans loved it—and learned something from it. Always an excellent rider, Jay participated in professional harness racing. As with everything, he performed brilliantly, running in hundreds of races and winning his share.

In the sixties we worked together now and then in television commercials, like those for Geno's Pizza, written by the hilarious satirist Stan Freberg. Those ads were great fun, and I really treasured the chance to perform with Jay again.

But even when we weren't working together, we continued to see each other socially. His family would come to our house for a barbecue, or ours would go to his place in Canoga Park for dinner.

Jay had a stroke in 1974 and was never in good health after that. He was presented with a star on the prestigious Hollywood Walk of Fame for all of his contributions to film, television, and radio. I was so proud to hear about that. He deserved the honor if anyone did.

In early 1980 he took a turn for the worse. I told his wife Mary that I would like to see him. She said, "He is not very well, Clay. I don't know if you would like to see him or not."

I insisted, "Yes, of course I want to see Jay." He was hospitalized at the Motion Picture and Television Home and Hospital in Woodland Hills. Mary met me there, and we went into his room. He looked bad. It was terribly heartbreaking. I leaned over the bed and said, "Jay, this is Clayton. Keep on fighting. We all love you." It was a terrible shock seeing him like that—so emaciated, such a shadow of the great man he had been. I don't think he even knew I was there.

A couple of weeks later, I was working a horse show in Dallas. When I flew home to California, my wife picked me up. I knew something was wrong as soon as I saw her. Sitting in the car, she said, "He's gone." I guess I knew who she meant, but I asked anyway.

"Who's gone?"

"Jay. He died yesterday."

He passed away on March 5, 1980. I went to his memorial service and said a few words. But how do you sum up a friendship like ours in just a couple of sentences? I could only hope that Jay, wherever he was, knew how much I loved and respected him and how much of an impact he had on my life and on so many other lives.

His body was cremated. The ashes were scattered over the Six Nations Reservation in Canada where Jay was born only sixty-two years earlier.

I miss Jay Silverheels a lot. He was a genuine, gentle man. We had an unbreakable bond of friendship from the first day I shook his hand in the spring of 1949 in the office of George Washington Trendle.

CHAPTER TEN

The Lone Ranger Rides Again!

I guess I never knew how much I had missed playing the Lone Ranger until I learned that there was a possibility that I might be able to do it again. From the day my agent, Earl McQuarrie, called me and said that Trendle was interested in having me come back, I began to feel a growing excitement. The serials and features I had done at Republic in the meantime had been amusing and educational. But there was a clear difference between just playing a part and actually inhabiting a role. The Lone Ranger offered so much to me that I couldn't find anywhere else. I was determined to get the job back if I could.

Just as I had never been told why John Hart replaced me, so I never learned why they wanted to get rid of him. Fans over the years have told me that John did a creditable job, but that they could just never accept him as the *real* Lone Ranger. I know that Trendle recieved a flood of mail on the subject, but I can't say that this was the reason they wanted to bring me back.

Earl McQuarrie told me that we were going to meet Trendle at the Beverly Hills Hotel. I dressed well, but casually, and tried to feel as much at ease as possible. I didn't want to appear too eager. We walked in and saw Trendle sitting in the salon. When he rose to greet us, I could see a curious look of shock on his face. As I shook his hand, he said, "Clayton, where's your beard?"

I had no idea what he was talking about.

"What beard?" I asked.

Trendle said, "Somebody told me that you had grown a beard."

"Well," I said, smiling and pointing at my chin, "I didn't."

He looked carefully at me. "Does this mean that you haven't been roaming around on Hollywood Boulevard quoting Shakespeare, either?"

Now I was *really* flabbergasted. I said, "Did someone tell you *that*, too?"

"Yes," Trendle said. "I thought you had become a lunatic."

I couldn't imagine how such a strange rumor had gotten started, but I thought it best not to push the point. We sat down, ordered drinks, and started talking about the series. He didn't say anything about why John Hart was out or why they wanted me back. He just talked about my return as if it were a foregone conclusion.

What he also didn't mention was that he was negotiating, even at that moment, with oil millionaire Jack Wrather to sell the character of the Lone Ranger, lock, stock, and barrel.

I was back on *The Lone Ranger* set by early June 1954. It was like old times, working with Jay Silverheels, as well as many of the old crew members. If anything, things were better than ever. The new scripts offered me more opportunities to play different characters besides the masked man. I often played a comic Frenchman, Father Batiste; an old geezer; and even a circus clown. In one episode, "The Return of Don

Pedro O'Sullivan," which aired in October 1956, I played three separate roles, including a Mexican bandit and a red-haired Irishman. I loved doing these different parts. It kept the show interesting for me; there was always something enticing and fresh to try.

My first new episode aired on September 9, 1954. A month earlier Trendle had sold all rights to the show and the Lone Ranger character to Jack Wrather for $3 million, in cash. It was the highest price ever paid for a radio or television property.

Overnight we had a new boss. Jack Wrather was three or four years younger than I was, friendly and personable, and a brilliant businessman. When I look back at what he accomplished in his life, I'm stunned: He produced not only *The Lone Ranger* but the television hits *Lassie* and *Sergeant Preston of the Yukon*. He built the Disneyland Hotel, founded the PBS station KCET, and turned the Queen Mary and Howard Hughes's experimental airplane, the *Spruce Goose*, into tourist attractions in Long Beach. And these were only a *few* of his accomplishments. I admired him as a man and as a tycoon.

When Jack took over, he came to me one day and said, "Clayton, is there anything you want to discuss, any changes you want to make in the show?"

I was gratified that he wanted my input. And, yes, there was something I wanted to discuss. Just before I was released from the show in 1952, the mask suddenly became much larger. I now believe that this was done deliberately because they knew they were going to replace me and wanted a mask that would hide John Hart's face as much as possible, in hopes that the fans wouldn't notice that a new actor had taken over the role.

"Jack," I said, "I would really like for the mask to be made smaller. This larger mask has always seemed to me like something an outlaw would wear. I don't think it's appropriate for the Lone Ranger."

He thought about it for a moment. "You know, you're absolutely right," he said. "I want you to get with the wardrobe people and get a mask that you think is just right."

That's just what I did. I admired that about Jack. He was the boss and could have ordered me to do whatever *he* wanted. But he knew that I only wanted the best for the show, and he valued my opinion enough to ask me about things. Such cooperation makes for a wonderful working relationship.

Jack's wife was actress Bonita Granville. She starred in several of the movies he produced and was my co-star in *The Lone Ranger* feature in 1956. She was a lovely person, easy to work with, and talented. Being the boss's wife, she could have thrown her weight around on the set, but she was always generous and cooperative—just one of the gang.

Whenever ownership changes hands, you always worry about what changes are in store. In this case, every change was for the better. Remember the story I told earlier about that tongue-twisting line, "This is just a trick that Trigger Taylor tried to pull?" I begged to have that line changed so that I could say it easily, but they refused. Trendle always wanted every line delivered precisely as written. I never had this problem with Jack Wrather. I could always talk matters over with him. If my solution made sense, he was happy to make a change.

Also, I now had the opportunity to fine-tune the Lone Ranger. Trendle's idea of the character was to make him very stoic, an almost unemotional champion of justice with the strength of a dozen men. He pursued that image for years. After my return I made the Lone Ranger more believable, more of a human being. He feels pain. He pats a kid on the head and knows how the kid feels because he was once a kid himself. I loved Trendle's original conception of the character—I just wanted to make the Lone Ranger a bit more human.

The biggest difference between my years with Trendle and with Wrather can be summed up this way: I always called George Trendle "Mr. Trendle." I always called Jack Wrather "Jack."

We filmed a lot of the exteriors in *The Lone Ranger* at Old Tucson, an atmospheric old movie town in Arizona. We did most of our sound stage work at Hal Roach Studios and at a supermarket on the northeast corner of Robertson and Pico. Wrather had rented or bought the place and converted it into a big sound stage. Later we relocated to General Service Studios at Las Palmas and Santa Monica Boulevard. That was a great place to work. We shared a sound stage with Ann Sothern's comedy series *Private Secretary*. Lucille Ball and Desi Arnaz also worked on that lot.

We had an open set, so anyone could just walk right in. Chuck Connors used to come over, looking for work. He ached to land a part in *The Lone Ranger*; I don't know why they didn't hire him. He was only doing bit parts at the time. I wish I could say that when I met Chuck, I knew he was going to be a television star, but that's something you can never foresee in this business. Of course, within a couple of years he was starring in *The Rifleman*, one of the biggest hits on television.

My good pals Rand Brooks and Tris Coffin appeared in several episodes of *The Lone Ranger* during this period, and I also had the privilege of working with such great performers as Lyle Talbot, good old Roy Barcroft, Slim Pickens, Virgina Christine, Whit Bissel, and many others. In the episode "Return of Dice Dawson" from July 1955, I worked with Harry Carey Jr. (whose nickname was Dobie). His father had been one of my favorite cowboy stars when I was a boy, and it was a real treat to meet his son. Of course, Dobie carved out an impressive career for himself, appearing in such classic films as *Three Godfathers* (1948) and the movie that I consider my favorite Western, John Ford's *She Wore a Yellow Ribbon* (1949).

While some things changed under Jack Wrather, others stayed the same. We still worked with low budgets, although I think the overall production values improved slightly. If you watch several episodes of the show back to back, you'll almost certainly notice "the Rock," a huge prop boulder that appeared in scene after scene. The prop men carried it around with them almost everywhere we went. We had another green set at General Service Studios. That's an interior set made to look like the outside. I don't think our green set fooled anybody. There was a Western street at General Service also, so we didn't necessarily have to go on location for an exterior shot.

Lone Ranger fans may not be aware that there were actually two Silvers. The first one was the horse we called Liver Lip because of his protruding lower lip. He had a dark spot on his hindquarters that had to be dyed white before filming. The second one came along while John Hart was starring as the Lone Ranger. Though it was rarely visible on the show itself, horse two had a black spot in his left ear—the only black spot he had on his body. That's how I can always tell the number one horse from the number two horse in photographs today. Otherwise, they were nearly identical.

Neither Silver was my personal horse, of course, but I made sure they were taken care of, well bedded down, and handled with kid gloves. I kept a pretty close eye on those horses. We sometimes went on tour together, and I had special rubber horseshoes made so we wouldn't damage schools' wooden stages. If Silver and I did a parade, I would use steel shoes with borium nails—much harder than steel. I never took number one horse on tour. Both were specially trained for motion pictures, but Silver number two was very camera wise. Sometimes we used a motor to start the camera, and his ears would twitch when he heard it; he knew when the camera was on.

All of the horse work Tom Steele and Dave Sharpe taught me at Republic came into great use on *The Lone Ranger* shows. I performed all my own running mounts and as much of the horse work as I could get away with. I could remember how awkwardly I had ridden in *The Perils of Nyoka* back in 1942, but now I felt totally in command as a rider and enjoyed it immensely.

Beginning in 1956, something new was added to *The Lone Ranger*—color. At this time few people in America had color television sets, but the number was growing. I believe Jack Wrather wanted to make sure that our program could continue to show in reruns for years to come. Other shows, like *Superman* and *The Cisco Kid*, were also converting to color. Walt Disney was shooting many of his shows in color, even though they were originally broadcast in black and white. That shows how smart Disney was. Those programs are still being broadcast and enjoyed by new generations of kids today, over forty years after they first aired.

The production methods of *The Lone Ranger* didn't change much because of color, but I think the shows immediately looked more impressive. We did a little more location work than usual, just to get the brilliant blue of the sky, the green of cactuses, and the red-brown of the desert sands. We went north, filming at beautiful Lone Pine and Sonora, California, and east to Kanab, Utah. We still worked at the usual places, of course—Iverson's Ranch, Corriganville, and Gene Autry's Melody Ranch, but traveling to more distant scenic areas gave *The Lone Ranger* the spark of something new.

I don't think it had anything to do with our new color photography, but this was also the same season that *The Lone Ranger* went into international release. We had already been broadcast in Canada for some time, but now we were seen on the British Broadcasting Corporation (BBC) in England. Later on I would travel to Great Britain to find that our fans over there loved the Lone Ranger just as much (and just as loudly) as American fans did.

⋈

I had often wondered why George Trendle wasn't more serious about making the Lone Ranger a hit in movies as well as on radio and television. Aside from the serials in the thirties, there were no big-screen adventures of the Lone Ranger. Maybe Trendle felt that his other *Lone Ranger* markets were profitable enough. When Trendle sold the rights to *The Lone Ranger* to Jack Wrather, the television show was showing on fifty stations nationwide, and the radio show was being broadcast on 249 stations. The comic strip ran in 300 newspapers, and *The Lone Ranger* comic books sold 2,000,000 copies per month. There were *Lone Ranger* toys, clothing, souvenirs, and memorabilia of all kinds. I guess Trendle just didn't think that he needed the movies.

But Jack Wrather was anxious to take the adventures of the Lone Ranger and Tonto to the big screen. *The Lone Ranger* feature went into production in the summer of 1955 at Warner Brothers Studios in Burbank. Directed by Stuart Heisler, written by Herb Meadow, and produced by Willis Goldbeck, the film was a first-class adventure for all of us. Jack's wife Bonita Granville was also in the picture, as were Lyle Bettger, Bob Wilke, and Lane Chandler.

The greatest thing about working on the feature was that the pace was much more leisurely. On the series, we would shoot at least twelve pages of script a day, sometimes as many as fifteen to eighteen, but for the film, we would shoot maybe four or five. That's still working pretty fast compared to some productions, but it seemed like a vacation to us.

The film was also better creatively. The pace allowed us to take the time to make sure everything was right, that we were well rehearsed and ready to do our best. You could really get your adrenaline going on the television show, which gave you a certain kind of energy, but it was a real plus to be able to think things through.

I remember several incidents during the making of *The Lone Ranger*. In one scene the Lone Ranger is shot and wounded (this was filmed in Bronson Canyon). I was supposed to grab onto Silver's stirrup and he would drag me to safety. For some reason they became concerned that Silver number two would kick me while I was down beside his feet. So they brought back Silver number one—good old Liver Lip—for that one scene. He was a real pro and did the drag just perfectly.

The Lone Ranger also contains what I consider to be

one of the great fight scenes in Western movies. My double, Bill Ward, had a terrific set-to with stuntman Bob Morgan. Bill leapt from Silver's saddle over to Bob's horse, and from there they went rolling down this steep hillside, slugging away the whole time. I remember watching and thinking, "These guys are going to be killed!" It really looked great. Those stuntmen seemed almost superhuman to me sometimes. Unfortunately, Bob Morgan lost a leg a few years later, doing a stunt during a runaway train scene in *How the West Was Won* (1962).

We filmed on location in Kanab, Utah, a beautiful setting for Westerns. We enjoyed working there immensely—except for one incident. We were in a canyon doing a scene. Jay Silverheels was there. So were Bill Ward and several crew members, including Stuart Heisler. Engrossed in our work, we suddenly heard a low rumbling sound. We were connected by radio to a unit farther up the canyon, and we received a frenzied message:"Flood! Get out of there!"

It was a flash flood that had started who knows where. We scrambled up the slopes as quickly as we could, carrying whatever equipment we could grab. About a quarter of a mile north, there were several generators and all kinds of sound and camera equipment—it all came tumbling toward us in that roaring mountain of water.

It ended almost as quickly as it had started. We just sat there, looking at an amazing path of destruction. Thousands of tons of water, under terrific pressure, had forced its way through that canyon in a matter of minutes. If any one of us had been caught in it, we would have been swept away to certain doom. When it was over, it was almost as though we were waking from a dream.

They ordered us out of the location immediately. I remember walking up to the main road and waiting for a car to take us back to our hotel. But we didn't stay away for long—we had a movie to shoot. We were back in the canyon the next day. An interesting aside, someone there had the presence of mind to keep a camera rolling, so footage of this flood exists. Personally I think Jack Wrather missed a good bet. He should have had a flood scene written into the picture to take advantage of the film he had of this near disaster.

We were all proud of the way *The Lone Ranger* turned out. Reviews were good and audiences were happy. In fact, it was on the list of the 100 top money-making films of the year. I still enjoy watching it today.

I had always done personal appearances to help publicize *The Lone Ranger*, but when the feature was released, I embarked on my longest tour ever—thirty-three cities around the country. I took Silver along, and we were greeted at every stop with real warmth and enthusiasm. Lassie came along, too—after all, that beautiful collie was a Wrather property just as the Lone Ranger was. In fact, Bonita Granville Wrather produced the *Lassie* television show. Also on the tour was the Western singing group the Riders of the Purple Sage.

We appeared at fairgrounds, schools, auditoriums—every place you could gather an audience. I would ride in on Silver shouting "Hi Yo Silver!" I would do a gun-twirling act, Silver would do a dance, and if circumstances permitted, I would answer questions from the audience and sign autographs.

Audiences in Asheville, North Carolina, got an unexpected bit of drama the night we performed for them. We were at a fairground at night, and the grass was wet with dew. When I reared Silver up, he slipped on the grass and came crashing down on me, dislocating my knee. I was in real pain, but my first thought went to Silver. I prayed he hadn't hurt himself seriously in the fall. Luckily he was fine. I wasn't, however. I had to make my next few appearances on crutches.

When we appeared a couple of weeks later in Charleston, South Carolina, I made a grand entrance riding in an orange Cadillac. I still walked a little gingerly, but I was no longer using the crutches. Silver and I were still able to do our act—just not together. Within a few days, though, I was riding my white stallion again.

⧓

One day while filming a *Lone Ranger* episode, I was working on a fight with a stuntman. He slammed me up against the wall, rocking it hard. A picture that was hanging there began to fall, and I caught it just before it hit the floor. When the prop man came to hang the picture back on the wall, I took a good look at it and thought, "Gee, that's a beautiful picture." I had just started to get kind of interested in antiques and realized that this picture wasn't painted on canvas. I asked the prop man what it was, and he explained that it was porcelain.

The prop man turned out to be very knowledgeable on the subject. Sally and I had already collected a few little porcelain plaques. When I told the prop man that I would like to try and find a painting just like this, he said he thought he knew where he could obtain one for me.

He was as good as his word, and within a day or two, I owned a beautiful porcelain painting. Fred Brannon, one of my directors over at Republic and a great pal of mine, was an expert on these antiques. One night Sally and I were out at the Brannons' house for dinner, so I showed him my new piece. When he took it apart, I could tell he was very im-

I'm in the Lone Ranger
costume minus the hat
and mask, 1949.

Scout, Tonto, the Lone Ranger, and Silver, ready for action.

Jay Silverheels and I with an unconscious Martin Milner, later star of *Route 66* and *Adam 12*, in "Pay Dirt," episode number twenty-eight (March 23, 1950). Note that I am still wearing the larger mask of the Trendle years.

James Arness, later the star of *Gunsmoke*, looks up to me in my large mask in a *Lone Ranger* episode called "A Matter of Courage," first broadcast April 27, 1950.

Silver and I during the production of *The Lone Ranger* feature (1956).

Tonto (Jay Silverheels) gets tough with a bad guy in the feature film *The Lone Ranger* (1956) as Jack Picard *(second from right)* and I look on.

A dramatic scene from the feature film, *The Lone Ranger* (1956).

Here I am as an old geezer in *The Lone Ranger* feature (1954).

Jay Silverheels *(left)* and I as clowns in the *Lone Ranger* episode "Wanted: The Lone Ranger."

In makeup as Shakespeare's Othello in the final *Lone Ranger* episode, "Outlaws in Greasepaint."

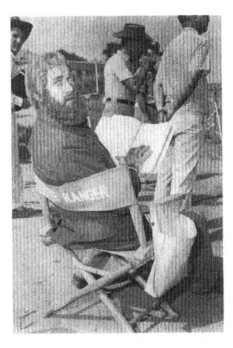

Clayton Moore, character actor

A happy day. Sally and I bring home our new daughter, Dawn Angela, in December 1958.

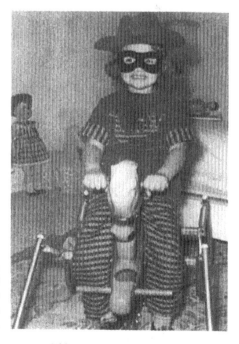

Four-year-old Dawn, following in Dad's footsteps, riding a Silver of her own in November 1962.

I was mobbed by fans during my 1958 tour of the British Isles promoting *The Lone Ranger and the Lost City of Gold.*

Fans line up for autographs in a London department store in 1958.

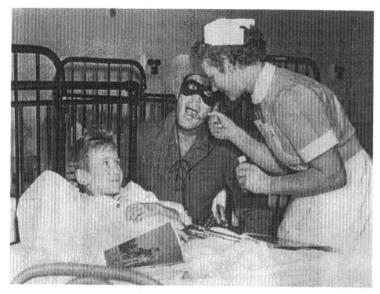

I show a young patient how to take his medicine in a Liverpool, England, hospital in 1958.

In Glasgow, Scotland, with three lucky contest winners in 1958.

In Washington D.C. with Treasurer of the United States Ivy Baker Priest in 1958.

Me with Vice President Richard M. Nixon in 1959, promoting the United States Peace Patrol.

Me, Dale Evans, and Roy Rogers at the Los Angeles Coliseum in the mid fifties.

Chuck Connors, John Wayne, and myself on a show celebrating ABC-TV's Silver Anniversary. The program aired February 5, 1978.

At the Los Angeles Press Club in 1980, fielding questions about my fight to retain the right to wear the mask.

Taping a television special, "The Cliffhangers," with Leonard Maltin.

At the wedding of
my daughter Dawn
to Michael Gerrity
(left) August 31,
1990.

Clarita and I cut the cake after our wedding at Dawn's home. We said our vows
on January 18, 1992.

I celebrated my eightieth birthday at the Gene Autry Western Heritage Museum, with a 1916 portrait of myself and my brothers Sprague and Howard *(right)*.

Douglas Fairbanks Jr. and I chatted about the old days in Hollywood at the Lone Pine Film Festival in 1992.

Receiving my star on the Hollywood Walk of Fame in 1987.

Mine is the only star on the Hollywood Walk of Fame with the names of both actor and character.

"I *am* that masked man!"

pressed. He told me that I had a KPM plaque in an English Florentine frame. "This is a real winner," he said.

As I said, Sally and I had already started collecting antiques on a casual basis, but this piece intensified our interest. Soon we were collecting cut glass, antique plates, ruby glass, cranberry glass, late and early Victorian pieces of all kinds.

I became especially interested in acquiring clocks: cuckoo clocks, grandfather clocks, chime clocks, pendulum clocks. My collection eventually included over forty of them from the Victorian period to the present. During an earthquake in 1958, every clock in our Tarzana house stopped exactly at midnight, just as the ground began to rumble. We were really shaken by the quake. Its incredible noise was made even louder and stranger by the bonging and clanging of forty antique clocks. I remember waking up suddenly and feeling as though I were inside a clock repair shop that was being bombed—a most unusual sound.

That quake also knocked about twelve inches of water out of my pool. Our house looked like a disaster area. Although I loved the antiques, I was most concerned about the safety of my family and my buckskin horse. Luckily everyone was fine.

That buckskin was a real favorite of mine. I only owned two horses in my life—this big buckskin horse, Buck, and a little quarter horse, Mergatroyd (don't blame me; that name was his when I bought him). Tarzana, more rural than it is today, was a splendid place to ride the horses. There was a great trail alongside the train tracks, secluded and rustic, like having a nice ride in the country.

When I was the Lone Ranger, everyone assumed that the white horses belonged to me and the studio didn't discourage that notion. They weren't mine, of course, but I worked out Silver number one very often. The second horse, bought for John Hart, stayed with Glenn Randall, a great stuntman and horse trainer; Glenn was also Roy Rogers's trainer.

✂✂✂

The last new episode of *The Lone Ranger* aired on June 6, 1957. Called "Outlaws in Greasepaint," it was about actors who use their traveling show to cover up bank robberies. The Lone Ranger and Tonto set out to capture them, naturally, and in the course of the investigation, I got to play a Shakespearean actor made up as *Othello*. I always loved it when the script gave me one of those enjoyable departures, as in an earlier episode, "Wanted: The Lone Ranger," when both Jay and I appeared as circus clowns.

I mourned the ending of the show; *The Lone Ranger* had truly become a part of my life. Since 1949, I had appeared in 169 of the 221 episodes. (John Hart starred in 52 shows.) And I already knew that no other role would ever match this one.

For the time no other role had to take its place. I was in Reading, Pennsylvania, on tour with Silver, when one of Wrather's associates, Bill Shay, called me with good news. "Clay," Bill said, "you need to fly back to Hollywood for a couple of days."

"Why?" I asked.

"We're going to do another feature film, and we need you and Jay to come and look over the script and talk things over with Jack," he said. "Then you can go back and finish your tour."

I was delighted. I knew that the first feature, *The Lone*

Ranger, had been a big hit, and I had hoped we would get to make another.

"Hey Bill," I said. "What's the name of this one?"

Bill replied, "*The Lone Ranger and the Lost City of Gold.*"

"It sounds great," I said. "I'll be there the day after tomorrow."

Jay and I met with Jack Wrather later that week. He gave us copies of the script written by Robert Schaefer and Eric Friewald. Both of us liked it very much.

Here's the plot of this one, according to the press book:

> The Lone Ranger (Clayton Moore) and Tonto (Jay Silverheels) learn that some hooded riders have been murdering Indians near the town of San Doria.
>
> The leader of the raiders, Ross Brady (Douglas Kennedy), and his girl friend, Frances Henderson (Noreen Nash), see a threat to their plot to steal five medallions which when put together reveal the location of an Indian lost city of gold.
>
> Chief Tomache (John Miljan) has given five pieces of the medallion to five of his friends and relatives, three of whom have now been killed. The Lone Ranger takes it upon himself to save the two survivors, a grandson and a nephew. He is too late to save the nephew who is killed by one of Brady's henchmen.
>
> As a result of the Lone Ranger's getting hot on their heels, Brady and Frances have a falling out, and she kills her boyfriend as the Lone Ranger and Tonto come upon them. They take Frances into custody, and the lost city of gold remains with its rightful owners—the Indians.

This time the director was Lesley Selander, a veteran of fast-paced Westerns and adventures since 1936. Les had worked frequently with Hopalong Cassidy, as well as other Western stars, Gene Autry, Buck Jones, Tim Holt, Russell Hayden, Richard Dix, and many more. Working with Les was akin to working with old pros like Bill Witney. Jay and I knew we were in goods hands.

Our cameraman was Kenneth Peach. He used a camera device that really sped things along: a crab dolly. In those days cameras moved on tracks just like miniature railroad tracks. If a character was walking down the street, they would lay tracks beside him so the camera would roll along with him. Camera tracks are still in use today, of course, but this crab dolly was a real improvement. It was a wheeled platform that held the camera on the end of a crane. The cameraman could move it around fluidly, going from long shot to close-up without much trouble at all.

I remember at least one scene in *The Lone Ranger and the Lost City of Gold* that must have been four or five pages long—Les Selander and Kenneth Peach captured it all in one take. If they had broken it down into individual shots, having to set up the camera here and there for different angles, it would have taken us all day to get this scene on film.

The Lone Ranger and the Lost City of Gold opened with a sequence that explained the origin of the Lone Ranger. We were all pleased with the way that scene turned out. Later, when all thirty-nine color *Lone Ranger* episodes were repackaged into thirteen features (each edited from three original shows), this sequence was added to the beginning of every one. During this precredit sequence, audiences heard a brand new song, "Hi Yo Silver," by Les Baxter and Lenny Adelson. The song was released as a single and sold well. I've heard that the original 45 rpm records are very collectible today.

The Lone Ranger and the Lost City of Gold was extremely popular with the show's fans, and Jay and I were proud to have been connected with such a fine production. We were also quite sad. Although neither of us was through with the characters yet—not by a long shot—we would never again appear in film or on television in adventures about the Lone Ranger and Tonto.

CHAPTER ELEVEN

England and a New Daughter

I was accustomed to going out on the road and making personal appearances as the Lone Ranger, but when *The Lone Ranger and the Lost City of Gold* opened in 1958, I learned that I was about to make one of the great journeys of my life—to the British Isles.

I didn't know what to expect. I knew that *The Lone Ranger* television program had been airing on the BBC in England for over a year and that it was very popular, but I had always heard that the British people were cold and reserved. I didn't know how these proper people would greet a masked man.

The moment I stepped off the plane, I knew how wrong I was to worry. Meeting me at Heathrow Airport was a cheering throng, thousands of excited kids and adults as eager to make the acquaintance of the Lone Ranger as any American audience I had ever seen. This enthusiasm continued throughout the entire tour. In fact, I remember a policeman in Cardiff saying to me with a smile, "I'll be glad when you get out of here, so we can get the trains running again."

Just as in the States, I always wore the Lone Ranger costume and mask whenever I appeared in character. But not the *entire* costume—I had had to leave my guns at customs. No one is allowed to bring firearms of any kind into Great Britain. A few months earlier I had visited the White House and Vice President Nixon and had worn my guns on that occasion. It's funny to think I could take guns into the White House and not into England. The guns were returned to me a few days later, however, just in time for a big party the BBC threw for me.

I conducted my personal appearances in England in much the same way as I had in the States—telling the story of the Lone Ranger, twirling my pistols, and answering questions from the audience. I guess I shouldn't have been surprised when the questions were much the same as I always got. My answers, however, sometimes got different reactions.

One time after the usual questions about Tonto and myself and the mask and the guns, a girl stood up and asked if I were married. I waited a long beat before answering.

"I'm the *Lone* Ranger!"

The audience laughed uproariously. Then I got a laugh I didn't intend. A young boy got up and said, "About your horse Silver, what does he weigh?"

I told him, "Silver weighs 1,250 pounds."

This time the laugh was bigger than before. I was baffled. I turned to the master of ceremonies and asked him why they were laughing. He explained that in Great Britain, the word *pound* only refers to money, never to weight.

"Oh," I said, turning to the audience. "Well, in case anyone is interested, Silver is worth much, *much* more than 1,250 pounds!" And they went wild again, laughing and applauding.

I later told Jay Silverheels that he would have been very interested in one of the sights I saw on my trip to the British

Isles. We were being entertained by the Duke of Bedford at his magnificent ancestral estate, Woburn Abbey. Deer wandered through the woods surrounding the Abbey. The stags had beautiful, large branching horns. Then I was shocked to see bison browsing on a wide, green lawn. I was told that the herd was larger than any existing in captivity in America.

The British people were fascinated by the Lone Ranger, of course, but I was keenly interested in them, too. I was not only interested but touched by some of the sights I saw. We visited many children's hospitals where I found a wonderful spirit among the patients, and such camaraderie between them and the nurses. One of the most impressive hospitals was the Princess Margaret Rose in Edinburgh, modern and new, with moveable glass walls at the ends of the wards so that the patients could be wheeled out into the sunshine and open air when the days were mild enough.

The children in those sad hospital wards knew the Lone Ranger and were tickled to meet him. But I felt as though *I* was the one receiving the lion's share of blessings by meeting these brave, wonderful, optimistic kids.

I recall an unforgettable incident that happened on the Thames. While in London, we took several river trips—I was just enthralled by the Thames with its magnificent docks and picturesque bridges. So many different kinds of boats and crafts moved up and down the river constantly, and I never tired of watching them go about their business. One Sunday afternoon, as we boarded the ferry, we noticed a group of young nurses with children from Dr. Bernardo's, one of the London hospitals we had visited.

Now I usually only went out in public in my Lone Ranger costume, but on this Sunday I was wearing a business suit. I figured no one would recognize me anyway. To my amazement one boy took one look at me and shouted, "I know you! You're the Lone Ranger!" I was flabbergasted, but I went straight over to him, knelt beside him, and talked awhile. The boy had no arms and legs and I'd noticed him particularly when we were at the hospital. I was impressed with his pluck—he was trying out his artificial legs so proudly. It was heartbreaking and inspiring all at once to spend time with children like these.

The three young nurses, I found out, were on volunteer work. They regularly gave up their Sundays to care for the children, who were allowed to choose the place of their outing. This day they had chosen a trip on the Thames. I could understand why, for the river had me completely under its spell. I swore then that I would return to England some day to explore the Thames, to make canal trips on a barge, seeing the English country in a leisurely manner.

I noticed that England, like the rest of the world, was losing some of its old landmarks, which were falling in the path of progress. Modern shopping communities and housing projects were replacing village life; modern touches, so common in America, were threatening the charming antiquity that made England so attractive. It was sad to see lovely old buildings, quaint streets, and villages being effaced. In America we marvel at buildings a hundred years old. In Great Britain many places we visited dated back centuries, even to the days before William the Conqueror landed. Of course, nearly forty years have passed since my trip there, and England has, I'm certain, been even more modernized. I suppose part of my fondness for the American West is a nostalgia for the way things used to be. Progress isn't all bad, but I wish there were a way to retain at least some of the charm and simplicity of the past.

Our tour of the British Isles went to Cardiff, Newport, Swansea, Stratford-upon-Avon, Edinburgh, Glasgow—all in a week and a half. Of these, Stratford was of particular interest to me. I'd never performed Shakespeare, but I had always loved his plays, having read most of them over the years. I was impressed to stand in the place where he lived.

From Glasgow, we journeyed to Belfast. If I thought the reception in England was enthusiastic, I was completely unprepared for the way we were greeted in Ireland. I had to be given a bodyguard, a powerful young man who stood about six-foot-six and weighed upwards of 300 pounds. He was a heavy, muscular, stout fella. We did the stage show at the opera house. Before the show the manager of the theater came to me and said, "Mr. Moore, you had better go out on the balcony and wave to the people of Belfast who have been waiting to see you but who couldn't get tickets." I was happy to do so but didn't expect such a throng. I stepped out on the balcony and waved to what must have been thousands of people who could not get into the theater. It was quite a feeling.

After the show I had to exit out the front door. A policeman stood on one side of me and the bodyguard on the other. The policeman said to me, "Mr. Moore, I want you to put your arms around my waist." Graham Edlebute, a publicist who worked for Jack Wrather and was traveling with me, was told to stay behind me, holding onto my guns. The policeman said, "We will break our way through the crowd." With that he just bullied right through—everyone just had to step out of the way. We got into the car. The people were very physical; they would take their little kids and put them up against the glass. It was a little nerve-wracking.

I returned to Los Angeles on August 15, 1958. The trip

had been unforgettable, but I was returning home to an experience that would turn out to be the greatest thing that ever happened to me. In December 1958, Sally and I adopted a baby girl. We had thought for a long time about what we would name our baby when she arrived. One day we were looking through a book of names, and we came across one that we loved—Dawn. Beside it were the words "new day, new life." How perfect, we thought. Our wonderful baby would be the start of a new day and a new life for all of us. We named her Dawn Angela.

As I look back over an eventful and pleasurable life, I have to say that the single happiest moment was when a nurse brought Dawn into the sitting room of the Children's Home Society and handed her to me. I looked at Sally and she said, "What do you think?"

I said "She is the most beautiful thing I ever saw." Sally said Dawn looked like a little China doll.

We had wanted to adopt a child for some time and had experienced all the trials and tribulations of anybody who wants to adopt. We were interviewed repeatedly and our backgrounds were checked thoroughly. It was frustrating sometimes, but we were happy to do it. We knew that such a process was the only way to make sure children went to good homes where they would be loved and cared for.

I remember at one meeting the social worker interviewed Sally and me individually. We were asked, "If you had a little child and she had a doll and threw the doll on the ground and kicked it, what would you do?"

I thought about it for awhile and said, "I would go pick up the little doll and hand it back to the child and say, 'I know you don't want to hurt your doll. Give it a big hug to show that you're sorry.'" I never did find out how Sally answered the question, but the adoption people must have been satisfied with both our answers.

When they asked if I'd rather have a boy or a girl, I told them that I wanted a boy. However, they decided not to give me a boy because they thought that, being the Lone Ranger, I would be too strict on a son. They believed it would be too difficult for a little boy to live up to my expectations. Of course, from my first look at Dawn, I was so completely delighted and pleased that it never bothered me one bit.

I still remember the day when we learned she was going to be ours. Mr. Rohr, the man who worked for the Children's Home Society, called us on the telephone early in December. He said, "I'm not going to send a Christmas card this year. We have a Christmas *present* for you." He was right. Dawn was the most wonderful Christmas present we ever received. She was four months old, born just about the time of my tour of the British Isles.

Being good parents was very important to us. Sally and I made it a point to keep Dawn out of the limelight when she was little. We didn't want her picture in the papers or anything else to prevent her from having a normal, happy, loving childhood.

In fact, when I was doing personal appearances, I always discouraged questions about my family. I didn't think it was fair to bring them into the public eye, unless they specifically wanted to be there. I was never rude to people, but if they asked personal questions, I always gently steered them back to the subject of the Lone Ranger.

It turned out that Dawn was a very talented singer with a great voice and a flair for mimicry. She did wonderful impressions of both Al Jolson *and* Barbra Streisand. Now that's versatility. There was a time when she wanted to pursue singing professionally, and Sally and I encouraged her. But she soon got a job as a clothes buyer for Bullocks Wilshire and decided against a career in show business. Dawn told me, "It took me about two seconds to figure out I didn't want to be put up for rejection. I am not the victim type." And, of course, she was right. In this business you hear a very emphatic "no" far more frequently than you hear "yes."

One time when Dawn was only a couple of years old, my friend Johnny Weissmuller came to visit us in our house in Encino. Johnny and I had just done a personal appearance together down South. I appeared as the Lone Ranger and Johnny as Jungle Jim (other actors had taken over the Tarzan character by then). We had known each other slightly back at the Illinois Athletic Club when we were kids but only ran into each other occasionally in Hollywood. I liked him, though, and always enjoyed getting together when circumstances allowed.

But I don't think Dawn has such pleasant memories of Johnny Weissmuller. This particular day it was very hot, and we decided to cool off at the pool. Johnny, of course, was an Olympic champion swimmer and was a marvelous diver as well. He had a special dive unlike anything I had ever seen. He could hit the surface of the water and hardly submerge at all, as though he were jumping onto the floor. While Dawn was watching, Johnny did this dive and then started shrieking like a walrus. I thought it was hilarious, but it scared the dickens out of Dawn. She ran screaming for her mother's arms.

In about 1964, Sally and I began to wonder if California was the best place for us to live. Since I no longer had any interest in performing on television or in films as any character but the Lone Ranger, there didn't seem to be much point in staying near Hollywood. I was touring the country regularly, making personal appearances of every nature, but this allowed me to live anywhere. Besides, as Dawn reached school age, we began to think about better parts of the country to bring her up.

Sally had grown up in Minneapolis, and many members of her family still lived there. We often visited the city and liked it very much. It seemed clean and safe and was far less expensive than Los Angeles. We talked it over with each other and with her family. It seemed like a good idea, so we moved to Minneapolis.

Once we were there, it also made sense to find a steady, stable job, so that I could spend more time at home with my wife and daughter. Sally's brother-in-law, Phil Pangras, suggested real estate. The idea appealed to me; after all, that's what my father and older brother did for a living. I was somewhat familiar with the business, and I liked Phil and thought we could work together.

That's how we came to form Ranger Realty. We were going to sell property and build homes. I studied in Minneapolis and received my Realtor's license, but that's as far as things got. Ranger Realty never really materialized.

So I continued to make my living through personal appearances. I booked shows out of Minneapolis and traveled to all parts of the country. I enjoyed meeting the fans, but I regretted the long weeks I had to be away from Sally and Dawn. I would often try and make it up to them with gifts. I remember I once brought Dawn a pair of hamsters back from one of my tours. These hamsters absolutely hated each other. One finally killed the other one, and Dawn gave the survivor to her kindergarten class.

We liked Minneapolis, but only stayed there a few years

before returning to California. However, we never gave up the idea of finding a better place to raise Dawn. In the early seventies a friend suggested Lake Tahoe, a clean, beautiful place without the crime and drug problems of Los Angeles. After we checked it out, we moved there so Dawn could complete high school in Lake Tahoe. Of course, it turned out that the community had the same problems of cities everywhere. I guess there's no place you can go to escape the negative aspects of modern life.

CHAPTER TWELVE

Adventures on Television

Because *The Lone Ranger* first went on the air in 1949, I guess you could say that I'm a television pioneer. I was around when the medium was truly in its infancy, and I've watched styles and technologies grow and change over the years.

We filmed *The Lone Ranger* as though it were a feature picture—only with shorter schedules and lower budgets. When we blew a line or something else went wrong, we just did another take. Because of our low budgets, we were always encouraged to get it right the first time, but if we didn't, it wasn't a disaster.

But many other television programs of the day were live. If an actor on a live telecast forgot his line or bumped into the backdrop or broke a prop, the show had to go on. There was no stopping, no doing it again. It was just like live theater —opening night every night. In fact, live shows often had to be done twice, once for the East Coast and once for the West Coast three hours later. In the days before videotape, the only way you could record a live broadcast was to point a 16 mm movie camera at a video monitor and film it right off the screen. These were called kinescopes, and it's only because of them that we can now see the great early television productions like *Playhouse 90*, *Omnibus*, or the memorable variety shows with Sid Caesar, Milton Berle, and Jack Benny. However, thousands of those shows are now gone, never to be seen again.

It is fortunate that *The Lone Ranger* was shot on film. That means the episodes look as good today as they ever did, providing that each negative is well preserved.

While *The Lone Ranger* was on the air, I kept guest appearances on other shows to a minimum. I was a guest villain on *Hopalong Cassidy* in the early fifties, but otherwise, the only television shows I appeared in besides *The Lone Ranger* were local children's shows when I was on tour.

For that reason, I didn't have much contact with live television—except for one memorable performance on *The Ed Sullivan Show*. By the time it was over, I never wanted to do a live show again.

When the *Sullivan Show* asked me to be a guest, Jack Wrather was delighted at the possibility of such good publicity. I believe *The Lone Ranger and the Lost City of Gold* had just been released, and *The Ed Sullivan Show* was one of the most popular variety programs on the air. Sullivan wanted to do a little skit with me, so Wrather had his writers come up with a script.

I've spent so much of my life performing that I've never felt too nervous when I'm about to go on, yet I recall feeling butterflies in my stomach while waiting in the wings of Sullivan's New York theater. After all, Sullivan and I hadn't rehearsed together and there could be no retakes. Everything—good or bad—would be seen instantly by literally millions of people.

I was in costume, of course, and Jack Wrather and Monty Livingston were sitting in the front row. Sullivan was supposed to talk about Silver and Tonto, ask me about *The Lone Ranger* show and the new feature, and then lead me into a gun routine. My appearance on the show was preceded by considerable publicity. As I stood in the wings, hundreds of calls started coming in, asking when I was going to be on. A stage manager walked over to me and said, "I wish Sullivan would hurry and put you on. The lines are all tied up because of you."

They must have tied up the lines for nearly an hour because I didn't go on until next to the last act, which was an acrobatic act. Now I always thought you put the biggest act at the very end, but Sullivan was going to finish up with these acrobatics.

Finally, with his trademark stiff gestures and odd voice —the delight of mimics for years to come—Ed Sullivan introduced me. The response was very enthusiastic from the large studio audience. Sullivan chatted with me about this and that—never touching on the script at all and never leading me into the gun routine. I started to feel flop sweat. I didn't know how I was going to exit the stage. So I just did a short routine anyway, twirling the guns. I was supposed to end by handing the pistol to Sullivan and, as he reached for it, snapping it into my holster. Then he was to ask me to give him the pistol, and he was going to do some funny business with it, then we were through.

Well, I turned the gun over to him, and he reached for it. Just as we planned, I pulled it back and did a snap put-away. And he never said a word. I stood there waiting for him to ask for the gun, but he did nothing. He messed up the routine completely.

I don't even remember how I got off the stage. Sullivan headed for his dressing room. Jack Wrather later told me that he and Monty Livingston went to Ed Sullivan's dressing room, but Sullivan had a security guard at the door who wouldn't let them in.

Later Monty and Jack came to my hotel, and as soon as I opened the door I said, "*Never* put me on a live show unless you have control of it." Of course, we all knew that anything could happen in live television, but I never expected things to go quite so wrong.

Most of my other television experiences were more positive. In 1958 when I was touring the country publicizing the Lone Ranger Peace Patrol, I performed several shows. I remember one enjoyable appearance with Minnie Pearl, as well as a children's show in Minneapolis with the memorable title, *Kangawoowoo*. It was a local show hosted by Bob Gordon.

A while later I appeared on the popular game show *What's My Line?* The premise of the show was simple, but a lot of fun. A celebrity panel tried to guess the occupation of guest contestants. Each person on the panel could ask one question at a time until they figured out what "line" the person was in. Pretty regularly they booked celebrity guests. On those occasions the panelists wore blindfolds, and the celebrity would disguise his or her voice.

Because I appeared in the costume and mask, they had to wear the blindfolds for me. I remember that Arlene Francis and Soupy Sales were on the panel. And nobody guessed who I was. Because I answered questions—only "yes" or "no"—in my old geezer voice, someone guessed Walter Brennan.

Just a few years ago, I had one of my most enjoyable

and nostalgic television appearances ever. ABC television produced "When the West Was Fun," a salute to television cowboys, and they invited all of us who were popular in the fifties and sixties. Chuck Connors was there. So were Pat Buttrum, Hugh O'Brian—everybody. I think my old pal Jock Mahoney was in charge of getting all of us to appear; he's the one who asked *me*, anyway. The special was narrated by Glenn Ford. The program turned out very well, but that was less important to me than the experience of shooting it. I had a great deal in common with all those other television cowboys, and we spent a long time talking over old times.

Something similar happened in 1995 when *Vanity Fair* magazine produced a special television issue. For one photograph, taken by famed photographer Annie Lebovitz, they gathered together an impressive bunch of old television cowboys. It was great to put on the Lone Ranger costume and mask and pose with Clint Walker, Fess Parker, Hugh O'Brian, Robert Horton, Robert Loggia, Gene Barry, Dale Robertson—and John Hart.

In the 1960s, a few years after *The Lone Ranger* had stopped production, Jay Silverheels and I were asked to appear in several television commercials. I have always been careful not to mock the character of the Lone Ranger or demean the image in any way. So if Jay and I decided that the commercials were funny and entertaining, and didn't make the Ranger or Tonto look silly, then we'd agree. Geno's Pizza were the most popular ads. Usually Jay and I just walked on at the end of the spot to deliver the punch line.

Because Jay was often working on his own tours or because he was ill, I often appeared by myself in commercials. I did a whole series for Aqua Velva aftershave and received cases of Aqua Velva for years after that.

Although I had reared Silver hundreds, if not thousands, of times, the people making the Aqua Velva commercial decided that a stuntman would handle the horse work at the end of the ad. They called in one of the greats, Hal Needham, who later turned from stunting to directing movies like *Smoky and the Bandit* (1977) and *Hooper* (1978). Needham was supposed to vault onto the horse. The horse was there by himself. Needham came running down a board about a foot wide and leapt, and the horse tumbled over backwards. Luckily neither Needham nor the horse was hurt. They tried it again, and this time, perfection.

I also did several amusing ads for Dodge cars, in which I appeared on a car lot, asked for a job in my Lone Ranger costume, then became a supersalesman. I believe those ads were so funny because I played the part absolutely straight—deadpan. Just standing there in the blue suit, white hat, and black mask while being a car salesman was funny enough. I didn't have to mug or make faces to get laughs. Those ads appealed to my sense of humor, kind of dry and understated.

One time I was in Peoria, Illinois, doing a Dodge commercial at one of the dealerships. I had just come from Minneapolis where I had appeared at a Dodge luncheon. The owner of this dealership received a call from one of the executives at the Dodge company in Detroit. The executive seemed agitated and wanted to talk with me immediately.

I got on the phone with the man, and he said, "I've just been told that your car isn't a Dodge."

I said, "No sir, it isn't. My car is a Cadillac."

I was about to add that my *maxi-van* was a Dodge, but he had already hung up. He seemed perturbed.

Over the years I also did commercials for General Mills,

Corning Ware, and children's toys. I enjoyed the work. It didn't pay a great deal, but the ads didn't take long to shoot and helped to keep me active and in the public eye. Of course, today, celebrity endorsements can be worth millions of dollars, but I can remember doing commercials in the sixties that only paid me $500 apiece. I guess I really needed a better manager at the time.

I believe that I turned down only one commercial, which was for a popular brand of beer. I actually thought long and hard about this endorsement when it was offered to me and came up with a way that I could do it and still be true to the character. Here was my idea: Two men are seated at the bar. The swinging doors open up, and the Lone Ranger strides in. The bartender says, "I'm a little taken aback to see a man in a mask. What will you have, stranger?" I reply in a tough voice, "Milk!" The two fellows sitting at the bar look at one another and back to the Lone Ranger. The Lone Ranger drinks the milk down, leaves a silver bullet on the bar, then walks out.

The advertisers didn't go along with this, however. They wanted to shoot a regular beer commercial. But I remained firm that the Lone Ranger could never be shown drinking alcohol. There's a big difference between having a little fun with the character and undermining everything for which the Lone Ranger stands.

These are just a few of my adventures with television. I hope there are still more to come. After all, nearly a half century has passed since the first time I stepped before a camera dressed as the Lone Ranger. Television and I have known each other too long to say goodbye now.

CHAPTER THIRTEEN

You Don't Pull the Mask Off the Ol' Lone Ranger

After *The Lone Ranger* went off the air in 1957, and *The Lone Ranger and the Lost City of Gold* was released in 1958, I began to settle into a new career of personal appearances. With the exception of a single episode of *Lassie* in 1959, I never again appeared publicly as any character but the Lone Ranger. The *Lassie* episode was a special occasion, of course, because the show was owned by Jack Wrather and produced by Bonita Granville Wrather. I thought the world of both of them and was happy to appear on their show.

But personal appearance tours were my bread and butter from that time on. I would sometimes do as many as 200 live shows a year. On occasions I performed my gun-twirling, story-telling, question-answering act. On others, I was a master of ceremonies or simply a guest of honor, there to meet and greet my fans at shopping mall openings, fairs, and amusement parks. In every town I visited, I would always make it a point to visit hospitals and orphanages to entertain the children. I didn't get paid for those kinds of appearances except in the most precious currency of all, the smiles of kids.

The questions at all the appearances were the same: Is the Lone Ranger married? Who does the cooking when you're out on the range with Tonto? Someone would always ask, "Do you ever take off your mask?" and I would answer, "Only to wash my face."

It was a good living and suited me well. I enjoyed traveling and seeing fans from all parts of the country. And, of course, I loved portraying the Lone Ranger under any circumstances.

Since the Wrather Corporation owned the rights to the Lone Ranger, I paid them a fee every time I received money for one of my appearances. It was a good system that benefited both Wrather and myself. Of course, I always had it in the back of my mind that the public would like another *Lone Ranger* television series or feature film. I kept myself in tip-top physical shape, always ready to step before the cameras again.

Little did I know that Jack Wrather also thought a new film would be a good idea. The only problem was that his plans did not include me.

⋈

One day in 1975, my agent, Art Dorn, received a call from Stanley Stunnel, one of Jack Wrather's top executives. "Art," he said, "Are you and Clayton Moore free for lunch tomorrow?"

"Sure," Art replied. "What's up?"

"We'll talk about it at lunch," Stunnel said.

They agreed that we would meet at Wrather's office on North Canon Drive in Beverly Hills and walk to a restaurant from there. If the whole setup struck Art as odd, he didn't say anything. I went to the lunch assuming that we were going to discuss a business proposition.

The next day, as Art and I stood in the lobby at the Wrather Corporation, waiting for Stanley Stunnel, Jack Wrather came walking through. He seemed a bit surprised to see me.

"Oh, Clayton," Jack said, "you're going to have lunch with Stanley, aren't you?"

"That's right, Jack," I said.

He acted a little distracted and obviously wasn't interested in further conversation. "Good, good," he said, walking away.

Stanley Stunnel arrived, and the three of us strolled to a nearby restaurant. After only a few moments of small talk, Stanley got to the point.

"Look," he said, "you're going to have to stop billing yourself as the Lone Ranger."

That felt like a slap in the face. It was a moment before I could speak. "What do you mean?" I asked slowly.

Stunnel said, "The Wrather Corporation owns the rights to the Lone Ranger, and you are breaking the copyright by appearing as that character. We want you to stop immediately."

Art started to explain that I had been making my living for nearly twenty years by going on tour in the Lone Ranger costume. But Stunnel wasn't interested.

"You've been doing this for too long," he said. "You can't make any more appearances as the Lone Ranger. If you do, we will have no recourse but to take legal steps."

I was just stunned. Our meals had just arrived, but I stood up. "Come on, Art," I said. "Let's get out of here." We walked out.

The next day Art Dorn drafted a letter that both of us signed. It stated that I would continue to make personal appearances, but instead of billing myself as the Lone Ranger, I would bill myself as "Clayton Moore, the man who played the Lone Ranger." We thought that would satisfy the letter of the law.

Unfortunately, the Wrather Corporation didn't see things that way. We began receiving regular legal threats ordering me to discontinue any public association whatsoever with the Lone Ranger. Of course, I refused to do this. I was more in demand than ever. Audiences around the country welcomed me as the man who played the Lone Ranger. To stop doing these personal appearances would have caused me great personal and financial distress. It was the way I made my living. More than that, it was the way I lived my life.

As time went on, I learned why the Wrather Corporation wanted me out of the way. They had a new feature film in preproduction, *The Legend of the Lone Ranger,* and planned on introducing a young unknown actor in the role. They felt that if I made personal appearances as the Lone Ranger, it would confuse the public. I thought that was ridiculous— audiences were smart enough to know the difference between me, the man who had played the part since 1949, and a young fellow who had never put on the mask before.

Besides, I had always realized that the day would come when a younger man would have to step into my shoes. I won't live forever, but the character of the Lone Ranger will. But I thought that the only way to introduce a new character was for me to pass the mask on. I even had a scenario for such a film. Here's the way I told it to a reporter in 1981:

Tonto dies, and I find a young man who is on the fence between going bad and standing for what is right and just.

There's a lot of good in him, but it needs to be developed. I take him under my wing, and we fight the forces of evil together. At the end of the film, after he's proven himself, I give him my silver bullets, and with my back to the camera, I take off the mask and hand it to him. I advise him to find a faithful companion to help him in his work, and tell him the task of seeking justice is now his. I ride off into the sunset, and the new Lone Ranger says, "Hi Yo Silver! Away!" as the *William Tell* Overture wells up. It would have been beautiful.

In fact, I *still* think that would have been the perfect way for the character to change hands—every Lone Ranger fan would have loved it.

But I found out that *The Legend of the Lone Ranger* would start right back at the beginning and recount the original massacre of the Texas Rangers, the survivor's introduction to Tonto and Silver, and all the other aspects of the Lone Ranger story. I felt as if I were being swept under the rug. After more than two decades of faithful service, I was being told to go away and pretend that I never had any association with the Lone Ranger.

Things got worse and worse for me. In the summer of 1979, Joel Boxer, Wrather's attorney, called me into his office. It was among the most humiliating meetings of my life. He told me I was too old to keep making personal appearances as the man who portrayed the Lone Ranger. Everything he said was insulting. A few days later the Wrather Corporation got a restraining order forbidding me to wear the mask. I was in shock.

However, if they thought I was going to roll over and play dead, they were wrong. I have always been a fighter, and since I knew that I was in the right, that just made me fight harder.

Bad things always seem to come in groups. At the same time that my whole professional future was thrown into question, Sally was feeling quite ill from the effects of diverticulitis. We hired a full-time nurse to care for her, but Sally's welfare was always on my mind. My upcoming legal problems were made all the more troubling because of my endless concern for her health.

Of course, Sally was a fighter, too. She always stood beside me, no matter how bad things got or how low either of us felt. I had always treasured her strength of spirit, never more so than during this dark period.

On August 17, 1979, a hearing was held on the subject of the restraining order. I arrived at the courthouse that morning with Art Dorn and our attorney, Bob Michaels. We had met on several occasions in Bob Michaels's office prior to this court hearing. During one of these meetings, Bob told me the Wrather people were telling the press that I was too old and too fat to portray the Lone Ranger. That statement was not only insulting but at least partly wrong. I then weighed about fifteen pounds less than I had when starring as the Lone Ranger on television. And through constant exercise, every day of my life, I was in great physical condition. Too old? That was a matter of opinion, I suppose. But I felt more than capable of playing the part better than I ever had.

During the hearing, in fact, the Wrather attorneys argued that I was "no longer an appropriate physical representative of the trim 19th-century Western hero." Later, when I was on the stand, I stood up, opened my coat, and asked the judge and the assembled crowd, "Do I look too fat to you?"

When we first arrived that morning, Art Dorn and I sat down in the back row of the courtroom. When the judge came in, he looked up and said, "Would the gentleman in the back row remove his white hat?" I stood up and walked out of the courtroom. To me, the white hat was a symbol of justice and law and order, and I felt there was no reason for him to ask me to take it off. Good guys wear white hats. Rather than make an issue of it, I walked out of the courtroom with Art Dorn; we stayed outside until it was time for me to be called to the stand. What went on in the courtroom while I was outside, I do not know.

But I read in the newspaper that one Wrather lawyer said, "It's our mask. By wearing the mask, Moore is appearing as the Lone Ranger. But in spite of what Mr. Moore feels in his heart, he is not the Lone Ranger. We own the Lone Ranger."

The hearing lasted for a couple of days. Bob Michaels tried to explain my position and how much the Lone Ranger meant not only to my own livelihood, but to my many fans around the country. This must have had some effect on the judge, who thought long and hard about the matter—we waited in the courtroom for more than three hours—then excused himself from the case. I heard that he was a Lone Ranger fan and didn't believe he could be impartial in the matter. The next judge, the Honorable Vernon Foster, had no such doubts. On August 30, 1979, Judge Foster ruled in favor of the Wrather Corporation. From that day forward I could not wear the mask or represent myself as the Lone Ranger in any public setting.

It felt like a slap in the face. I told a reporter, "I am astonished that this would happen. But I'm a fighter. I believe in that which is right. . . and the truth is I have been the Lone Ranger for the past thirty years and I will not give up the fight and I love my public and I'll fight for you—I'll continue to make personal appearances for my thousands of fans."

Art Dorn said, "Here's a company that feels they have the

right to tell Mr. Moore what he can and can't do as far as earning a living. As long as America is free, nobody has that right. We believe that he has a right to keep on portraying the hero that everybody has grown to love."

I have always tried to live up to the Lone Ranger code—fair play and honesty. And that made the removal of my mask unpleasant. It wasn't that I was angry. I just felt that the kids of our country were given a bad deal. The mask was the symbol of justice, law, and order, and they took me to court and issued a restraining order that took that symbol away.

However, I had no animosity toward the Wrather people. I just hoped and prayed that they would live up to the moral code that I had dedicated myself to ever since 1949.

The press reported around this time that I had been offered $150,000 to appear in a cameo role in *The Legend of the Lone Ranger*. That was false. I was never approached to be in the film. If I had been, I would have turned it down. It isn't that I had anything against the project personally, but I was completely uninterested in playing any part other than that of the Lone Ranger. I thought Klinton Spilsbury, the young man they cast in the role, was very handsome. He seemed to have the potential to be another Gary Cooper. But *The Legend of the Lone Ranger* had no interest for me; I didn't pay much attention to it at all.

As stunned as I was over the whole legal issue, I believe I was even more hurt about the damage to my friendship with Jack Wrather. It would be going too far to say that we were pals, in the sense that I was pals with Rand Brooks or Tom Neal, but Jack and I had a good relationship from the beginning. While we shot the television series and the two feature pictures, everything was fine between us. I liked him and Bonita. But he never talked to me about the mask. He had his executives and lawyers deal with me, and I never saw or talked to Jack. He never contacted me, nothing. I was angry for a little while. Then I felt only sadness that I had lost a friend.

Besides, the whole issue had arisen so suddenly. Throughout the sixties and most of the seventies, I never once heard from anyone in the Wrather Corporation that I should not be going on tour in character. Now, out of the blue, they wanted me to cease and desist.

But I guess I'm just not the cease and desist type. "All right," I said to myself, "if I can't wear the mask, I'll just have to make do with something else." I don't know when it occurred to me that wrap-around sunglasses might work, but I soon started searching for just the right kind. One day I was walking past a ski store in Encino. Glancing in the display window, I saw the perfect sunglasses—large, very dark lenses and wide earpieces. I went in immediately and tried them on. It wasn't an exact match for the Lone Ranger mask, but when combined with a cowboy costume, white hat, and six-guns, I thought it would be an effective substitute. I bought three or four pair right away.

I could have simply continued to tour as myself, Clayton Moore. But after years of keeping the mystique alive, it seemed wrong to just drop the veil. I hated to think of disappointing the fans. Besides, no matter what the restraining order said, I had no intention of just giving up the Lone Ranger. I knew that right was on my side and I would continue to fight until I could once again legally appear in character.

I'm happy to say that the fans accepted the compromise without complaint. Mask or glasses, they didn't care as long as it was Clayton Moore. Everywhere I went, people would insist, "You *are* the Lone Ranger!"

In fact, the public support soon became overwhelming. As soon as the country became aware that I had lost the mask, the most amazing and wonderful things started to happen. The city councils across California—in Valejo, Carson, Beverly Hills, maybe a dozen others—began adopting resolutions stating that Clayton Moore was the official Lone Ranger and that I had a right to earn my livelihood through the character. All over the country, fans began circulating petitions demanding the mask be returned to me. Art Dorn told me that there were eventually more than a million names on those petitions. In fact, when the restraining order was reported in the papers, Art said that he received more than 250 phone calls in a four hour period. "I'm just inundated," he said at the time. "I can't get off the phone. It's absolutely incredible." Grassroots movements started springing up everywhere with slogans like "Save the Lone Ranger" and "Keep the Mask On." I appeared on more than 250 talk shows in just a few months. And I received nearly a half-million passionate, supportive letters like these:

> I am 47 years old, a member of one of those generations (and there are several) that grew up with and still identify Clayton Moore as THE Lone Ranger. The ethics of the Lone Ranger are unquestionable. He is a legend whose standard is more than just Law and Order: it is JUSTICE.
>
> For myself, I always had the impression that the Lone Ranger had at one time been a Texas Ranger. But for reasons known only to himself and Tonto he chose to become an anonymous Champion of Justice, an unsung hero, unhampered by the restrictions of formal legal procedure and thus able to provide the legal authorities with law-breakers of unquestionable guilt.
>
> Clayton Moore as he looks today even *more* personifies the image of the Lone Ranger; a man of experience and

knowledge who stands out as a hero in the battle of Good vs. Evil.

The Lone Ranger Inc. may get some cheap publicity for their new series [sic] but it would certainly be unjust to let them unmask Clayton Moore. We much prefer to let the good and simple recipients of the Lone Ranger's gentlemanly assistance continue to ask, "Who was that masked man?" We know it's Clayton Moore, but for the sake of justice and the code of the West, let's keep his secret!

><

I noted this week that the movie studios have a date in court with Clayton Moore, because they wish to strip him of the mask of The Lone Ranger.

I firmly believe that Clayton Moore should be allowed to remain as the Lone Ranger. He made the character become alive to millions of people and generations of kids. He lives the character and by doing so, he becomes the Lone Ranger.

Granted, every actor/actress who plays a role for a one-time film should not be granted the divine right to be forever that character when it was only a one-time deal and the character becomes forgotten. But when an actor/actress plays a particular role for most of his life and lives by the principles of the life of the character, then where do you draw the line of when the person stops being the character and the character stops being the person? They become one entity.

By removing the mask, you might as well cut out his heart and let him die. The people of the world would accept a dead Clayton Moore, rather than an unmasked one.

><

The names Clayton Moore and The Lone Ranger have been synonymous for most of my life. To ask Clayton Moore to turn in his mask is like asking all the Moms in America to quit baking apple pie.

The Lone Ranger is an American tradition and Clayton Moore the personification of that tradition. If the new owners of the Lone Ranger copyright remove Clayton Moore's right to wear the mask of The Lone Ranger, then I, for one, will never purchase any products made by them.

><×<

Next thing you know some big businessmen are going to take Santa's beard and boots away. Come on, America! What's this country coming to when the No. 1 Lone Ranger cannot ride again?

Personally, I grew up on the original Lone Ranger show and from time to time found myself in the lead role of the Lone Ranger in the local backyard game. Clayton Moore never objected to me wearing my mask and hat.

Whoever you are, big corporate weirdos, give us a break. Give The Lone Ranger a break. Hell, give America a break.

Money isn't everything. What about nostalgia?

><×<

The way the fans rallied behind me was so wonderful—I felt ten feet tall. It almost made the whole thing worthwhile to receive such unbelievable warmth, enthusiasm, and support from fans everywhere. To be able to feel so elated in the middle of such a painful episode was a rare gift.

In a way the Wrather Corporation did me a tremendous favor. My fears that the loss of the mask would affect my ability to make a living proved unfounded. In fact, the number of my personal appearances actually increased during that time, giving me additional opportunities to tour and see more of my fans. I realized that my fans were as interested in the real person behind the mask as they were in the Lone Ranger. That was very gratifying. And in April 1980, I began a long and happy association with the Texas Ranger baseball team, performing at their games and acting as their mascot.

One of the most moving things to happen during this

period was my 1980 appearance on the television show *Real People*. This popular program filmed a segment showing me at personal appearances, greeting my fans and signing autographs, and also interviewing people regarding their outrage at the way I was being treated. It was a rousing and sympathetic piece of film, and when it was over, the curtains parted and I stepped out onto the stage to join the show's hosts. The audience went wild, giving a long, loud standing ovation. The producers later told me that nothing like it had ever happened on the program. In fact, I never had a chance to say a word. The applause and cheering lasted so long they finally had to cut to a commercial. I kissed cohost Sarah Purcell and gave her a silver bullet, then stepped out into the audience and began shaking hands with the fans. It was one of the most thrilling things that ever happened to me.

All in all, despite everything, things were good, except for the missing mask.

Art Dorn, Bob Michaels, and I continued our legal fight to regain the mask. They met repeatedly with Wrather's attorneys. Every once in a while it would seem as if we were about to reach an agreement, but something always happened to put us back to square one. Bob even sued the Wrather Corporation on my behalf. I wasn't in favor of this, feeling that it would place us in a stalemate situation. But Bob was convinced that the countersuit was the only way to make the corporation take this issue seriously. Faced with defending themselves in court, perhaps they would simply lift the restraining order.

It didn't work out that way. I would not get the mask back for a long time.

The Legend of the Lone Ranger opened early in 1981. There's a show business saw that says, Any publicity is good publicity. But Lone Ranger fans across the country were so angered by my treatment during this whole ordeal that they stayed away in droves. I've been told that it's a respectable retelling of the story; some people even liked it a great deal. But I never wanted to see it, and never will.

When *The Legend of the Lone Ranger* bombed at the box office, many people expected me to feel smug and satisfied. But I would never wish failure on anyone. I had nothing against the people who made the film. The only satisfaction I received was the knowledge that the public had spoken loud and clear: "There is only *one* Lone Ranger —Clayton Moore."

In 1984 I was on a personal appearance tour when I opened a newspaper and learned that Jack Wrather had passed away. I was only a little shocked; I knew that he had had cancer. He had been placed in St. John's Hospital in Santa Monica, where he died on November 12.

Although Jack and I had not seen or spoken to each other since that brief encounter in his office in 1975 when Stanley Stunnel told me to stop wearing the mask, I was deeply saddened by his death. I remembered warmly my friendship with Jack and Bonita, and regretted that circumstances had separated us.

But Jack must have thought about me to some extent during his last months. The court case had been dropped on September 20, 1984, and about a month later, on October 17, Bonita Granville Wrather typed a note, which she sent to Art Dorn. "Dear Arthur," it read, "please be advised that Wrather Corporation hereby grants to Clayton Moore the rights to wear the Lone Ranger mask." Jack Wrather died about three weeks later.

Upon Jack's death, Bonita immediately took over the

company. On November 28 she was elected chairman of the board of Wrather Corporation.

I never spoke with Bonita about the lifting of the restraining order, so I don't know whether it was Jack's wish or hers that I be allowed to wear the mask once more. I like to think that they came up with it together and decided to make this final generous gesture of friendship. No matter which one of them thought of it, I was deeply grateful to both.

Actually I didn't find out that the restraining order had been lifted until some time in December. I thought it was a wonderful Christmas present. I made my first public appearance in the mask in New York in mid-January. On February 23, 1985, at the opening of a sporting goods company in Fairhaven, Massachusetts, I told reporters, "I'm so glad to have my mask back. It's my symbol, it's the Lone Ranger, and if I may say, it's Americana. I guess when I go up to the big ranch in the sky, I'll still have it on."

The year 1985 was a period of mixed emotions. My long fight to have the mask returned to me was over—I had won and was elated by my victory. But Sally's illness was progressing. Many days she suffered in terrible pain. Even at that difficult time for her, Sally was so supportive and loyal. She was even happier than I was that things had finally turned out well with the Wrather Corporation.

But in August 1985 she took a turn for the worse, and in early 1986 my wife of 46 years passed away. I was completely devastated. We had been so happily married for so long. I couldn't imagine life without her. I felt completely alone in the world.

In my grief, I made what turned out to be a mistake. In the final days of Sally's illness, her nurse Connie was very helpful and sympathetic to both of us. After Sally's death I turned to Connie for comfort, and in August 1986, six months after Sally died, Connie and I were married. Unfortunately, neither of us had married the other for the right reasons, and about three years later we divorced.

One night in 1990, I was at a party at the home of friends. They introduced me to Clarita Petrone, a widow who had recently moved to Palm Desert from Connecticut. Actually I had met Clarita on two previous occasions. In 1952 Sally and I had met Clarita and her sister Anita when they were visiting our next door neighbors, Amedeo and Rose Curcio, Dawn's godparents. More than twenty years later, Clarita and her husband were driving across the country. When they visited the Curcios again, Sally and I happened to run into them. I remembered her immediately, which shocked her a little, I think.

When her husband passed away, Clarita decided to move to California and bought a place in Palm Desert. When she needed dental work and was staying with the Curcios for a few days, I was invited over for a party one night, and that's how we ran into each other for the third time.

Clarita and I soon fell in love with each other and decided to marry. We were going to go to Laughlin, Nevada, or Santa Barbara for a small wedding, but my daughter Dawn suggested we get married at her home in Los Angeles. So on January 18, 1992, we did. It was a happy occasion—and it has been a happy marriage ever since.

I believe that I have had an eventful life, but the decade from 1980 to 1990 was probably the most tumultuous period of all, filled with highs and lows—illness, death, divorce, legal proceedings, the loss and return of the mask, and remarriage to a wonderful woman. I ran the emotion gamut during those years. It was exciting at some times, devastating at others. But I came out of it stronger, happier, and more secure than ever. Between you and me, however, I wouldn't mind if the decades to come were just a bit slower and duller.

CHAPTER FOURTEEN

The Adventures of Clayton Moore

As the Lone Ranger, I have always presented myself as a figure of law and order, of fair and honest dealings. That's what the character stands for, and that's what I've always stood for, too.

But all my run-ins with lawbreakers have not been on television.

One morning when Sally, Dawn, and I lived in Minneapolis—about 1964, I believe—I was walking to the supermarket that was about three blocks away from our house. It was cold and snowy. I was wearing a ski jacket and a hat with ear flaps—not exactly regulation Lone Ranger costuming. As I approached the market, I noticed through the window that a man was lying on the floor, just inside. He wasn't moving. I tried the door, but it was locked.

At that moment a lady came by. I told her, "There's trouble in the market. Please go call the police immediately." She hurried away to make the call, and I went around to the back of the store. The rear entrance was wide open. I cautiously made my way to the front. The man on the floor was the store manager. As a regular customer, I knew him pretty well.

And he knew who I was. He was gagged and tied up with electrical cord.

As I pulled the gag out of his mouth and started to untie him, I asked, "Are you all right?"

"Yes," he said. "I'm not hurt. Did you see anyone?"

He told me that two men had overpowered him as he was preparing to open earlier that morning. They had forced him to open the safe, then bound and gagged him.

It didn't occur to me until that moment that the men who did this might still be in the store. I said, "I'm going to take a look around." I also thought I should call the police again, in case the woman I spoke with earlier had been afraid to get involved.

So I headed back down the aisle to the rear of the store, where the manager's office was. The moment I stepped into the back room, two shotguns were shoved into my face. My first thought was that the robbers were still there and now *I* was in for it! But in the same instant, one of the men with guns shouted, "Freeze! Police!"

I was extremely relieved, even though the officers still suspected that I was the robber. I froze, just as they had ordered, and waited for the store manager to make his way to us.

"Is this the man who did this?" one of the policemen asked him.

The store manager smiled, "No, sir! He's the one who came in and untied me. Gentlemen, this is Clayton Moore—the Lone Ranger!"

I really didn't feel as though I had done anything heroic. I just happened to be the first person on the scene. I'd like to think that anyone would have helped out, given the same circumstances.

A few years later something similar happened. In August 1986 I was in Spartanburg, South Carolina, at a benefit for the South Carolina State Fireman's Association. My appearance was sponsored by a local children's show called *Appaloosa Andy*.

I had just finished a performance, and because there were a number of people at the stage entrance, I had decided not to change my clothes until I got back to the hotel. When I left the theater, I was wearing my mask and costume. I greeted the fans, signed autographs, and chatted a while as I made my way to the car.

A couple of blocks away from the theater, I saw an overturned motorcycle in the street and a man on the ground beside it. I got out of the car and went over to him to see what we could do to help out. My wife was a registered nurse, so she knelt beside him and checked him. She wanted to find out if he had a head injury as he was not wearing a motorcycle helmet.

My wife asked, "Are you all right?"

He mumbled something.

She said, "I want you to open your eyes and tell me what you see." She figured if he could recognize me, that would be a positive sign that he was thinking clearly.

He opened his eyes and looked at me. I said to him, "Do you know who I am?"

He said slowly, in disbelief, "The Lone Ranger?"

We laughed a little with relief. I said, "Maybe he thinks he's in cowboy heaven!"

The man's name was Pat Humphries. He said that he had been struck by a hit-and-run driver. While we waited for the police and ambulance to come, I directed traffic around the accident. I guess it must have been a startling sight—me with my mask, blue suit, and six-guns, acting like a traffic cop.

I'm happy to report Mr. Humphries was not seriously injured. The next day I stopped by his home to give him a photograph on which I wrote, "You're a very lucky man. Always wear your helmet, pard. Clayton Moore—The Lone Ranger."

As with the robbery in Minneapolis, I just happened to be the first one along to help, and I'm glad I was there. I think that it's good for kids to see that helping others is a way of living—both on television and in real life.

Those were both incidents in which I was lucky enough to be able to lend aid to someone in need. But there were two occasions when I was the victim of crime myself.

The first incident happened in June 1976, when I was in Lincolnwood, Illinois, a suburb of Chicago, appearing at the opening of a chain of discount stores. I had a van that I drove to all of my personal appearances, and when I arrived at the hotel there in Lincolnwood, I was told that it was too big to park in the regular lot. I was concerned about the van's safety if it were parked outside and unattended but was told that there was really no other option.

The next morning I discovered that I had been right to worry. As I carried my suitcase from the hotel to the van, I noticed that something was wrong. The door was dented. It had been forced open. Inside the van, all my belongings were strewn about—all my belongings, that is, that were still there. Thieves had taken several items, but the biggest blow was the loss of an antique 1833 Remington firearm. In terms of resale, the gun was valued at $1,200, but it was worth far more than that to me. The Remington was a beautiful piece; I had never used it on *The Lone Ranger* but frequently showed it off during personal appearances. Besides, it was a treasured part of my personal collection.

The thieves must have been surprised during their robbery. I carried a small outboard motor with me, in case I had time to rent a boat and fish. The motor was sitting on the passenger seat. They had moved it there but didn't take it for some reason. I also had a portable heater in the back. Behind it was a box filled with badges, turquoise Indian jewelry, some rings, and several coins—just things that I had collected along the way. The thieves certainly would have taken these things if they had spotted the box.

I was very angry at the theft—dishonesty of any kind infuriates me. I told a reporter, "There will be retribution!" But there wasn't. The revolver was never recovered or returned to me.

Several years later I had to go through the experience again, but with a more satisfying conclusion. On Christmas Eve, 1986, I had to fly into Houston, Texas for a personal appearance. Because you can't carry firearms onto an airplane, I had to check my chrome-plated pair of Colt .45-caliber revolvers. I placed their case inside a suitcase with a couple of Lone Ranger uniforms and other items. When we arrived in Houston, I got off the plane and headed for the baggage claim area.

I didn't get to the luggage carousel until after nearly everyone else had already picked up their bags and left. My suitcase was nowhere to be seen. I hoped that for some reason, it was just late in being unloaded, and so I waited a long time for my suitcase to appear. But it never did. Having an airline lose your luggage isn't exactly a rare experience, so I just assumed my bag had been accidentally rerouted to some other airport and that it would be returned to me by the end of the day. But all efforts to trace the bag failed; soon I had to face the fact that my belongings had been stolen.

Luckily there was a great deal of publicity about the theft. Only a few weeks later, I received a call from the Houston police. They had been contacted by Jack Hendlmyer, a local gun collector, who said that he had bought the guns from a Houston airline baggage handler! Apparently the thief had seen my bag circling the luggage carousel and had run off with it. As soon as Mr. Hendlmyer realized that he had purchased stolen property, he called the police and offered to return my guns to me.

The baggage handler was arrested immediately. My revolvers were returned to me in late January 1987. I never kissed a girl on *The Lone Ranger* show—I only kissed Silver—but when they handed my revolvers back to me, I kissed the guns.

I appeared at the trial of the thief in August 1988 and testified to the value of my twin Colts. I said that they were worth $20,000 on the market but were priceless to me. I had been using them on *The Lone Ranger* show since at least 1955. The trial didn't take long. The former baggage handler was placed on ten years' probation and fined $5,000. Also, he had to spend 600 hours cleaning up after the horses at the Houston Police Department stables. Retribution at last! However, I was never reimbursed for two Lone Ranger costumes and silver bullets that were never recovered.

I don't believe that the man who stole my guns was really bad; he was just a misguided man who, I hope, learned a valuable lesson from his punishment. But on one occasion in the late sixties, I brushed shoulders with true, chilling evil. Luckily I was able to walk away from these people with my life. There were others who were not nearly so fortunate.

A rancher, George Spahn, had a beautiful spread just above Iverson's Ranch. I knew George pretty well; he often supplied us with horses when we were filming in the area. I remember especially a little white mare we got from him for Chuck Courtney (the Lone Ranger's nephew, Dan Reid) to ride. Spahn did a little stunt riding in the movies and even built Western sets on his ranch, hoping he could lure the studios to use his place as a movie site. I never filmed anything there, but I believe a few low-budget films were made using George's sets and his ranch. By the late sixties it was used for little else than horse rentals.

In July 1969 I was in the area, showing Dawn some of the locations where we made so many Lone Ranger episodes, and decided to drop in and see George to say hello. My friend Jim Hoiby was with us, and we drove up to the ranch in Jim's Volkswagen van. When we arrived, we saw about a dozen young people on George's porch. They looked like hippies, which was not so unusual at that time. But it *did* strike me as a little unusual that they were here, on George Spahn's ranch. George Spahn had quite a few children himself, but these people didn't look like they even *knew* George, much less were related to him. I approached a couple of fellows and said, "I would like to see George Spahn. Is he here?"

One of the guys pointed over to a tiny, dilapidated trailer. "Over there," he said.

So we got back in the van and drove about a hundred yards over to the trailer. Inside, George was just sitting there motionless. It was very dark in the room. I called out, "George, how are you?"

He cocked his head toward me and said, "Clayton?" and began to cry. I didn't know until then that he had completely lost his sight. We talked for a while, and he seemed distressed. I really couldn't get him to say much. At one point a young woman[3] brought him a plate of food, and I said brightly, "It's lunch time, George!" The woman dropped the plate on the table beside his chair and shoved it roughly toward him. She didn't acknowledge Jim or me, and didn't say a word to George. Then she turned around and left.

We visited for less than an hour. George seemed depressed. As we prepared to leave, I said, "Is there anything I can do for you, George?"

He said, "Just come back to see me." I promised that I would. He sounded deeply lonely. But I never got the sense that he was in danger. If I had, I never would have left him there. He *was* in danger, though. I later learned that those young people were part of Charles Manson's "family"— Manson himself could well have been there that day. Only a couple of weeks after my visit to the Spahn Ranch, on August 9, 1969, some of these same kids brutally murdered Sharon Tate and several other people in one of the most horrible crimes of our era. I've often wondered if I had unwittingly taken my own life into my hands when I drove onto that ranch.

So many forces contribute to terrible acts like those of the Manson family. But when I read of the murders, I couldn't help but think that those murderers had once been innocent kids, who may have been fans of the Lone Ranger. How did

[3] This young woman may have been Lynette Alice "Squeaky" Fromme, who took care of Spahn. According to the book *Helter Skelter* by Vincent Bugliosi and Curt Gentry, Fromme hoped that Spahn would eventually will his ranch to her. That he never did so is probably all that kept him alive. An ardent follower of Charles Manson, Fromme later made headlines when she attempted to assassinate president Gerald R. Ford on September 5, 1975.

they take such a wrong turn in life? It made me more determined than ever to stand for decency, honesty, and compassion. If kids' minds are shaped by outside forces, I was determined that my influence, however small, would be for good, always.

CHAPTER FIFTEEN

Who Is That Masked Man?

During the terrible period when the mask was taken away from me and I was not allowed to appear in public as the Lone Ranger, I had occasion to think quite a lot about how much I had in common with this character. Because I fought so hard to keep the mask and to retain the right to make public appearances dressed as the Lone Ranger, some people probably think that I actually believed I *was* the Lone Ranger. Of course, that was never the case. I always knew I was playing a part, and there was and is a clear line between the character and myself.

Playing the part of the Lone Ranger changed my life. Before, I was just Clayton Moore. But once I put on the mask, I stood for so many good things. I had decided that if the Lone Ranger was going to stand for certain ideals, then I would have to live up to those ideals offscreen as well—otherwise, I would feel as though I was a hypocrite. Therefore, I've devoted myself—on and offscreen—to setting a good example for the young people of our country. The mothers of America want their children to be like the Lone Ranger. I want them to be able to point to me and say, "Look how straight he stands, how good his diction is, how neat his personal appearance is." I want to represent fair play, honesty, and love of country.

When I stopped appearing in *The Lone Ranger* series the first time in 1952, I was sad to leave the character behind. But I just went on with my career, playing different roles in different serials and feature films. When I returned two years later, though, I began to identify more closely with the Lone Ranger. Part of this feeling had something to do with my increasing contribution to the show—under Jack Wrather I was able to shape the Lone Ranger a little bit according to my own beliefs and point of view. Part of it came from the Lone Ranger Peace Patrol tour.

In 1958 I toured the country with the Lone Ranger Peace Patrol, a program to encourage youngsters to buy United States Savings Stamps. I met with Robert B. Anderson, secretary of the treasury, and Ivy Baker Priest, the treasurer of the United States. Most impressive, I went to the Capitol to talk with Vice President Richard M. Nixon. (I found him cordial and sincere—and a big fan of the Lone Ranger. I presented Mr. Nixon with some silver bullets to give to his young daughters, Julie and Tricia.)

Working in our nation's capital on a program that would help young people in so many ways made me look at the Lone Ranger in a different light. I had always known his potential to communicate good, healthy ideals through the television show, but now I realized that the Lone Ranger had great value *off* the screen as well. That's when it started sinking in that the Lone Ranger was more than simply a fictional character I portrayed on television. The things he stood for, I stood for. The things he fought against, I fought against. The ideals and code of the Lone Ranger made sense to me, and I made up my mind to live by them. As I once told a reporter, "I would like to have the Lone Ranger remembered as a great American, who was a friend to all. That he stood up for everyone, and that he epitomized everything that is great about America. And I would like for Clayton Moore to be remembered in the same way."

During the last year of the show, I became overwhelmed with the feeling that, no matter what, I wanted to continue to personify the Lone Ranger. I made a decision: even after production of the series ended, I would continue portraying the Lone Ranger. If there were no more television series or feature films in which to do that, I would simply do it on my own in personal appearances. I would go out and meet the public, the people who put me where I am.

And since 1958—the last time I played the role in a film, *The Lone Ranger and the Lost City of Gold*—that's exactly what I have done. I have appeared at countless nostalgia conventions, Western shows, rodeos, schools, and fairs. I have done charity functions, helped to open new stores, appeared at various fund-raisers. I tried to appear wherever there was an audience who wanted to meet the Lone Ranger. I talked a little and twirled my gun and answered questions my fans might have. After my friend Jay Silverheels died, I would talk about him, too, telling our fans what a great man he was, how proud he was of being an Indian—and how proud the American Indians were, and are, of him.

But although I always arrived at personal appearances with an act, mostly I just wanted to meet the fans and give them an opportunity to meet the Lone Ranger. These wonderful people have given so much to me, I felt that I should give something back.

But it was more than just deciding that I wanted to go on playing the Lone Ranger. I decided that I never wanted to play anything else—ever. I had found the role that suited me, that offered the most to me, and I would never confuse the issue by playing other characters. I've had a pretty strict attitude about this. In the seventies I was offered roles on *Happy Days* and *The Greatest American Hero*. Both programs wanted me to appear in the Lone Ranger costume for a cameo. In the first, I was to appear at a birthday party for Fonzie (Henry Winkler). In the second, a show which starred William Katt, they wanted me to ride Silver into a trailer and drive off pulling the trailer with a Cadillac—it was a little comedy thing. I turned them both down. I will only portray the Lone Ranger in a show or film *about* the Lone Ranger. Anything else, I'm not interested.

That also included, of course, *The Legend of the Lone Ranger* (1981). It wasn't that I thought it would be a bad film, or that it wouldn't be true to the ideals of the Lone Ranger. It was simply that I am only interested in playing the Lone Ranger, and nothing else.

I like to think of the Lone Ranger as something constant and steady in a society that is always evolving. Our country has been through so many changes, good and bad, over the past forty years, but audiences' responses to the Lone Ranger has never changed. In the midsixties I used to travel around the country in a camper, doing up to two hundred personal appearances a year. The kids who had first watched the show a decade earlier were now in college or were young adults. Some were hippies and war protesters. Others were students or soldiers on their way to or from Vietnam. It was an extremely turbulent, troubling time. But even though many of these kids had temporarily rejected many of their parents' values and dreamed of building a new society, they retained their affection and respect for the Lone Ranger. I was always greeted with a great deal of warmth and love.

The message of the Lone Ranger is a patriotic one, but even those young people who were not feeling very patriotic at the moment continued to have good feelings about both me and the character. I think one reason is honesty. At a time when young people felt as though they couldn't trust their government and when Native Americans were one of the minorities fighting to right the injustices of the past, the Lone Ranger remained a figure who was always honest and straightforward in everything he did and said. And his strong and wise Indian friend Tonto was a wonderful symbol of the dignity, intelligence, and compassion of this country's great native people.

Of all the hundreds of personal appearances I made over the decades, I was never heckled, never booed, never rejected. The overwhelming acceptance of audiences never ceased to warm my heart. Maybe it's hard to understand how such adulation can be humbling, but it was. I felt humble and grateful to be able to embody such wonderful ideals through the character of the Lone Ranger.

I've always had a positive response from law enforcement people, especially. And I in turn have a great deal of respect for the police department and everyone involved in law and order. Remember, when I was a child, I always wanted to grow up to be a cowboy or a policeman. That's why it was such an honor to be appointed a special officer of the police department of the City of Fresno, "in recognition of [my] outstanding contribution to law enforcement" on June 22, 1971.

The police have always been very kind and thoughtful

to me. On a number of occasions, men in uniform have come to my door to introduce themselves. I have often heard policeman say, "I sure hope my kids grow up to be like Tonto and the Lone Ranger."

Once, when Jay and I were making a personal appearance in San Francisco, we had dinner with a prison warden. I'll never forget what he said: "No boy is born bad. It is acquired." That's why I think our kids have to have as many positive influences as possible.

People by the hundreds have come up to me to say, "If it hadn't been for the lessons I learned from the Lone Ranger, who knows how I would have turned out?" That makes me feel so good and so proud. Others say, "I wish my children had heroes to look up to today like I had when I was a kid."

Of course, as the years go by, the Lone Ranger's audience gets older and older—and younger and younger. The original fans of Brace Beemer's radio *Lone Ranger* are now in their sixties and seventies. The baby boomers who first enjoyed our television version in the fifties are now nearly fifty themselves. It seems amazing to me that the oceans of kids who used to cheer as I would ride in a Christmas parade or step into the spotlight of a fairground, now have kids—and grandkids—of their own. But even though their hair is turning gray, they retain a childlike heart. The look in their eyes when they meet the Lone Ranger is the same at forty-five as it was at five. I know—I've met 'em both times.

And their kids and grandkids are now discovering the Lone Ranger and Tonto as well. The series has been running on television almost constantly for four decades. Today many episodes are available on video so that fans can watch them at home anytime they please. Even now, I meet little children, who haven't even started school yet, who are already enthusiastic fans of the Lone Ranger. They don't know that the shows were made when their parents were young—or before their parents were even born. All they know is that the shows are exciting and fun, and that the Lone Ranger and Tonto are true heroes.

Of course, not all kids today are familiar with the Lone Ranger. Westerns are not nearly as popular now as they were in the past. Today more kids would rather be in outer space playing with shock guns, not shotguns. This is not as much of a leap as people think—after all, didn't President Kennedy call space "the last frontier"? In the space shows, good still triumphs over bad, and some great lessons can be taught through these science fiction adventures. Nearly every episode of the series *Star Trek*, for instance, had a moral point to make, and fans of shows like that can absorb some fine ideas and ideals.

But I can't help but long for a real return to the Western. Westerns are true Americana. They tell of the struggles of our ancestors who came West seeking new homes, new ways of living, freedom and the promise of a bright future. The story of the West is inspiring and terrible, idealistic and bloody, sublime and atrocious. It embodies this country's best and worst characteristics. The good parts of the story inspire us. The bad parts warn us of what we have to do to make things better. Even though many Western films have only a slight connection to the true history of the West, I believe exposure to these motion pictures can stimulate kids to learn more about what their forefathers endured to make the United States one nation, from sea to shining sea.

I wish the kids of today knew more about the early pioneers and what they went through: rugged trails, starvation, traveling in terrible conditions of weather and in constant danger. I wish kids knew how the forests were conquered and the mountains were crossed, how families had to live for months in covered wagons, enduring great hardships, even death.

Western films and television programs can help to introduce this rich, colorful history, and I am heartened every time I see that a new Western has been made.

The Westerns of the past, of course, continue to have a large and enthusiastic audience. How my personal appearances changed over the years can attest to that. At first I was out greeting the fans of the *Lone Ranger* show. Now I greet fans who *remember* the show. Numerous motion picture conventions and Western shows around the country are attended by people who are so incredibly knowledgeable, not only about the Lone Ranger but about *all* Westerns. They tell me things about my career that I've forgotten, if I ever knew to begin with!

Many of the greatest honors of my life have come from groups and organizations dedicated to the Western films and film stars of the past. I was inducted into the Stuntman's Hall of Fame in 1982, and the following year I was given a Golden Boot Award at its first annual banquet attended by a "Who's Who" of Western personalities. I received the Western Heritage Award from the National Cowboy Hall of Fame in Oklahoma City in March 1990. And in October 1994 I proudly received the Gene Autry Western Heritage Award at a gala ceremony.

I received a star on The Newhall Walk of Fame, honoring my contributions to Western film and television. Newhall was a great movie location in the old days. Gene Autry's Melody Ranch movie set was there (actually it burned down several years ago, but it has since been rebuilt in a perfect replica, and movies are still produced there). That was a great thrill. Dennis Weaver (*Gunsmoke*) and Robert Conrad (*The Wild, Wild West*) were honored in the same ceremony.

But perhaps the biggest honor of all came in 1987 when I had a star placed on the Hollywood Walk of Fame. That came about because of radio announcer Rick Dees. He called me one day and said that he had learned that I didn't have a star on the Walk of Fame and that he was flabbergasted by the oversight. He knew that Jay Silverheels had received one several years earlier, just months before his death.

Although I am, of course, very grateful to receive honors, it never enters my mind to *want* one. I had never thought about the Hollywood Walk of Fame at all. It certainly didn't bother me that I was not represented there.

But it bothered my fans.

Rick Dees got his radio station, KIIS-FM in Los Angeles, to start a petition asking the Hollywood Chamber of Commerce to give me a star. It worked.

The day of the ceremony, the streets and sidewalks were crowded with people eager to share this moment with me. In fact, a whole tour bus filled with fans wearing masks drove by right in the middle of the ceremony! I was very moved when I saw the star itself. It reads: "Clayton Moore—The Lone Ranger." I have been told that it is the only star on the Walk of Fame that identifies both an actor *and* his character. I was elated, appreciative, and emotional. Remember, this was not long after the right to wear the mask had been returned to me. I had fought long and hard to identify myself with the Lone Ranger. Now here it was, in letters of brass, a permanent part of Hollywood history. Dawn picked the location herself, walking up and down Hollywood Boulevard, searching for the perfect spot. She finally found it, just across the street from the famous Chinese Theater—the heart of Historic Hollywood.

There was something else, too, that added to the deep feelings of that day. My wife Sally had been such a source of strength, happiness, and inspiration to me throughout our long marriage. I knew how much the honor would have meant to her. I know that she would have been so proud of what we accomplished—together. My wonderful daughter Dawn was with me, and I like to think that Sally was right there beside me, too, on that proud occasion. You can imagine the wide range of emotion I felt at that moment.

I spoke to the crowd, thanking them for their support over the years. I told them that this star was for them, more than for me. Then I turned to Rick Dees and said, "Thanks, buddy." That was quite a day.

But every day that I have spent with my fans is special to me. The love I have felt from generation after generation is more important to me than almost anything else.

At the end of almost every episode of *The Lone Ranger*, as Tonto and the Ranger would ride away, someone would ask, "Who *was* that masked man?"

At the beginning of my association with the role, if someone had asked me that question, I would have answered, "That masked man was the Lone Ranger, a fictional character from television, the movies, and comic books."

But today, after nearly half a century of connection with the role, my answer would be a little different:

"*I* was that masked man!"

It doesn't matter that I am Clayton Moore, an actor, and that the Lone Ranger is a legendary figure of folklore. In more ways than I can count, we have become one and the same. I have absorbed parts of him, and he has taken on the best elements of my personality. Until the day I am taken to that big ranch in the sky, I will continue to wear the mask proudly and to try my best to live up to the standards of honesty, decency, respect, and patriotism that have defined the Lone Ranger since 1933.

I have lived a long and happy life, filled with exciting events and interesting people. I have a loving family and many cherished friends. As an actor, I have played many roles that continue to be dear to my heart. But if I were to try to sum up my life and what it has meant, I can only repeat, "I was that masked man."

In fact, why speak only of the past? The truth is, I *am* that masked man!

Appendix

The Films Of Clayton Moore

FEATURE FILMS

The Cowboy from Brooklyn (1938) Warner Brothers
> Directed by Lloyd Bacon. Starring Dick Powell, Pat O'Brien,
> Ronald Reagan, Priscilla Lane, Ann Sheridan.

Go Chase Yourself (1938) RKO
> Directed by Edward F. Cline. Starring Joe Penner, Lucille Ball,
> Richard Lane, June Travis.

When Were You Born? (1938)
> Directed by William McGann. Starring Margaret Lindsay, Anna
> May Wong, Lola Lane.

Crime School (1938) Warner Brothers
> Directed by Lewis Seiler. Starring Humphrey Bogart,
> Gale Page, the Dead End Kids.

Radio Hams (1939) MGM
> A "Pete Smith Specialty." Directed by Felix E. Feist. Narrated by Pete
> Smith. Starring Jack Carlton (Clayton Moore), Eleanor Counts,
> Philip Terry, Barbara Bedford.

Sergeant Madden (1939) MGM
> Directed by Josef Von Sternberg. Starring Wallace Beery, Tom
> Brown, Alan Curtis, Laraine Day.

*Kit Carson** (1940) United Artists
> Directed by George B. Seitz. Starring Jon Hall, Lynn Bari, Dana
> Andrews, Ward Bond, Clayton Moore.

---

* available on home video

The Son of Monte Cristo* (1940) United Artists
>Directed by Rowland V. Lee. Starring Louis Hayward, Joan
>Bennett, George Sanders, Florence Bates, Clayton Moore.

International Lady (1941) United Artists
>Directed by Tim Whelan. Starring Ilona Massey, George Brent,
>Basil Rathbone, Gene Lockhart, Clayton Moore.

Tuxedo Junction (1941) Republic
>Directed by Frank McDonald. Starring the Weaver Brothers and
>Elviry, Thurston Hall, Lorna Gray, Frankie Darro, Billie Benedict,
>Sally Payne, Clayton Moore.

Black Dragons* (1942) Monogram
>Directed by William Nigh. Starring Bela Lugosi, Joan Barclay,
>Clayton Moore, George Pembroke, Robert Frazer.

Hello Annapolis (1942) Columbia
>Directed by Charles Barton. Starring Tom Brown, Larry Parks,
>Jean Parker, Thurston Hall, Phil Brown, Mae Busch.

Outlaws of Pine Ridge (1942) Republic
>Directed by William Witney. Starring Don Barry, Lynn Merrick,
>Noah Beery, Emmett Lynn, Clayton Moore, Forrest Taylor.

Cyclotrode "X"* (1946) Republic
>Feature version of *The Crimson Ghost*. See "Serials" for credits.

Heldorado (1946) Republic
>Directed by William Witney. Starring Roy Rogers, Dale Evans.

The Bachelor's Daughter (1946) United Artists
>Directed by Andrew Stone. Starring Gail Russell, Adolphe
>Menjou, Ann Dvorak, Jane Wyatt, Madge Crane, Clayton Moore.

Along the Oregon Trail (1947) Republic
>Directed by R. G. Springsteen. Starring Monte Hale, Adrian Booth,
>Max Terhune, Clayton Moore, Roy Barcroft, Leroy Mason.

El Dorado Pass (1948) Republic
>Directed by Ray Nazarro. Starring Charles Starrett, Smiley
>Burnette, Clayton Moore.

The Plunderers (1948) Republic
>Directed by Joseph Kane. Starring Rod Cameron, Ilona Massey,
>Paul Fix, Francis Ford, George Cleveland, Forrest Tucker,
>Adrian Booth, Clayton Moore.

Marshall of Amarillo (1948) Republic
>Directed by Philip Ford. Starring Allan Lane, Eddy Waller, Mildred
>Coles, Clayton Moore, Roy Barcroft, Trevor Bardette.

The Cowboy and the Indians (1949) Columbia
> Directed by John English. Starring Gene Autry, Sheila Ryan, Frank
> Richards, Jay Silverheels, Clayton Moore.

South of Death Valley (1949) Columbia
> Directed by Ray Nazarro. Starring Charles Starrett, Gail Davis,
> Clayton Moore.

Bandits of Eldorado (1949) Columbia
> Directed by Ray Nazarro. Starring Charles Starrett, Smiley
> Burnette, Clayton Moore.

Masked Raiders (1949) RKO
> Directed by Lesley Selander. Starring Tim Holt, Richard Martin.

Riders of the Whistling Pines (1949) Columbia
> Directed by John English. Starring Gene Autry, Patricia White.

Sheriff of Wichita (1949) Republic
> Directed by R. G. Springsteen. Starring Allan Lane, Eddy Waller,
> Roy Barcroft, Trevor Bardette, Clayton Moore, Lyn Wilde.

The Far Frontier* (1949) Republic
> Directed by William Witney. Starring Roy Rogers, Gail Davis.

The Gay Amigo (1949) United Artists
> Directed by Wallace Fox. Starring Duncan Renaldo, Leo Carillo.

Cyclone Fury (1951) Columbia
> Directed by Ray Nazarro. Starring Charles Starrett, Smiley
> Burnette.

Mutiny (1952) United Artists
> Directed by Edward Dmytryk. Starring Mark Stevens, Angela
> Lansbury, Patric Knowles, Rhys Williams, Peter Brocco, Clayton
> Moore, Morris Ankrum.

Buffalo Bill in Tomahawk Territory (1952) United Artists
> Directed by B. B. Ray. Starring Clayton Moore, Slim Andrews, Rod
> Redwing, Chief Yowlachie, Chief Thundercloud, Charlie Hughes.

Night Stage to Galveston (1952) Columbia
> Directed by George Archinbaud. Starring Gene Autry, Pat Buttram.

Captive of Billy the Kid (1952) Republic
> Directed by Fred C. Brannon. Starring Allan Lane, Penny Edwards,
> Grant Withers, Roy Barcroft, Clem Bevins, Mauritz Hugo, Clayton
> Moore.

Desert Passage (1952) RKO
> Directed by Lesley Selander. Starring Tim Holt, Richard Martin,
> Joan Dixon, Clayton Moore, Francis Mcdonald, John Dehner,
> Walter Reed.

Montana Territory (1952) Columbia
> Directed by Ray Nazarro. Starring Lon Mccallister, Preston Foster, Clayton Moore.

Barbed Wire (1952) Columbia
> Directed by George Archinbaud. Starring Gene Autry, Pat Buttram, Clayton Moore.

Hawk of Wild River (1952) Columbia
> Directed by Fred F. Sears. Starring Charles Starrett, Smiley Burnette, Clayton Moore.

The Raiders (1952) Universal
> Directed by Lesley Selander. Starring Richard Conte, Richard Martin, Morris Ankrum, Viveca Lindfors, Barbara Britton, Dennis Weaver, Clayton Moore.

Down Laredo Way (1953) Republic
> Directed by William Witney. Starring Rex Allen, Slim Pickens, Clayton Moore.

Kansas Pacific (1953) Allied Artists
> Directed by Ray Nazarro. Starring Sterling Hayden, Eve Miller, Barton Mclane, Douglas Fowley, Myron Healey, Clayton Moore.

The Bandits of Corsica (1953) United Artists
> Directed by Ray Nazarro. Starring Richard Greene, Raymond Burr, Paula Raymond, Clayton Moore, Lee Van Cleef.

The Black Dakotas (1954) Columbia
> Directed by Ray Nazarro. Starring Gary Merrill, Wanda Hendrix, John Bromfield, Noah Beery Jr., Jay Silverheels, Clayton Moore.

The Lone Ranger * (1956) Warner Brothers
> Directed by Stuart Heisler. Starring Clayton Moore, Jay Silverheels, Lyle Bettger, Robert Wilke, Bonita Granville, Lane Chandler.

The Lone Ranger and the Lost City of Gold * (1958) United Artists
> Directed by Lesley Selander. Starring Clayton Moore, Jay Silverheels, Douglas Kennedy, Noreen Nash, Charles Watts, Lisa Montell, Ralph Moody, Roman Frederic.

Justice of the West * *(1961)*
> Feature compilation of *Lone Ranger* episodes.

Appendix

SERIALS

The Perils of Nyoka * (1942) (also known as *Nyoka and the Tigermen*)
Republic
Directed by William Witney. Starring Kay Aldridge, Clayton
Moore, Lorna Gray, William Benedict, Tristram Coffin, Charles
Middleton, Forbes Murray, Robert Strange, John Davidson.

The Crimson Ghost * (1946) Republic
Directed by William Witney and Fred C. Brannon. Starring
Charles Quigley, Linda Stirling, Clayton Moore, I. Stanford Jolley,
Kenne Duncan, Forrest Taylor, Emmett Vogan, Sam Flint, Joe
Forte.

Jesse James Rides Again * *(1947)* Republic
Directed by Fred C. Brannon and Thomas Carr. Starring Clayton
Moore, Linda Stirling, Roy Barcroft, John Compton, Tristram
Coffin, Tom London, Holly Bane, Edmund Cobb, Gene Stutenroth,
Leroy Mason.

G-Men Never Forget * (1947) Republic
Directed by Fred C. Brannon and Yakima Canutt. Starring Clayton
Moore, Roy Barcroft, Ramsey Ames, Drew Allen, Tom Steele, Dale
Van Sickel, Edmund Cobb, Stanley Price, Jack O'Shea, Barry
Brooks.

Adventures of Frank and Jesse James * (1948) Republic
Directed by Fred C. Brannon and Yakima Canutt. Starring Clayton
Moore, Steve Darrell, Noel Neill, George J. Lewis.

The Ghost of Zorro (1949) Republic
Directed by Fred C. Brannon. Starring Clayton Moore, Pamela
Blake, Roy Barcroft, George J. Lewis, Eugene Roth, John Crawford,
I. Stanford Jolley, Steve Clark, Tom Steele, Dale Van Sickel.

Radar Men from the Moon * (1952) Republic
Directed by Fred C. Brannon. Starring George Wallace, Aline
Towne, William Bakewell, Roy Barcroft, Clayton Moore, Peter
Brocco, Bob Stevenson, Don Walters, Tom Steele, Dale Van Sickel.

Son of Geronimo (1952) Republic
Directed by Spencer Gordon Bennet. Starring Clayton Moore,
Roy Barcroft, Bud Osborn.

Jungle Drums of Africa * (1953) Republic
Directed by Fred C. Brannon. Starring Clayton Moore, Phyllis
Coates, John Spencer, Roy Glenn, John Cason, Henry Rowland,
Steve Mitchell, Bill Walker, Don Blackman, Felix Nelson.

Gunfighters of the Northwest (1953) Columbia
> Directed by Spencer Gordon Bennet. Starring Jock Mahoney,
> Clayton Moore, Phyllis Coates, Don Harvey, Marshall Reed, Rodd
> Redwing, Lyle Talbot, Tom Farrell, Terry Frost, Lee Roberts.

The Lone Ranger Television Episodes

SEASON ONE

1. "Enter the Lone Ranger" (9/15/49)
2. "The Lone Ranger Fights On" (9/22/49)
3. "The Lone Ranger Triumphs" (9/29/49)
4. "The Legion of Old Timers" (10/6/49)
5. "Rustler's Hideout" (10/13/49)
6. "War Horse" (10/20/49)
7. "Pete and Pedro" (10/27/49)
8. "The Renegades" (11/3/49)
9. "The Tenderfeet" (11/10/49)
10. "High Heels" (11/17/49)
11. "Six Gun Legacy" (11/24/49)
12. "Return of the Convict" (12/1/49)
13. "Finders Keepers" (12/8/49)
14. "The Masked Rider" (12/15/49)
15. "Old Joe's Sister" (12/22/49)
16. "Cannonball McKay" (12/29/49)
17. "The Man Who Came Back" (1/5/50)
18. "Outlaw Town" (1/12/50)
19. "Greed for Gold" (1/19/50)
20. "Man of the House" (1/26/50)
21. "Barnaby Boggs, Esquire" (2/2/50)
22. "Sheep Thieves" (2/9/50)
23. "Jim Tyler's Past" (2/16/50)
24. "The Man with Two Faces" (2/23/50)
25. "Buried Treasure" (3/2/50)
26. "Troubled Waters" (3/9/50)
27. "Gold Train" (3/16/50)
28. "Pay Dirt" (3/23/50)
29. "Billie the Great" (3/30/50)
30. "Never Say Die" (4/6/50)
31. "Gold Fever" (4/13/50)

32. "Death Trap" (4/20/50)
33. "Matter of Courage" (4/27/50)
34. "Rifles and Renegades" (5/4/50)
35. "Bullets for Ballots" (5/11/50)
36. "The Black Hat" (5/18/50)
37. "Devil's Pass" (5/25/50)
38. "Spanish Gold" (6/1/50)
39. "Damsels in Distress" (6/8/50)
40. "Man without a Gun" (6/15/50)
41. "Pardon for Curley" (6/22/50)
42. "Eye for an Eye" (6/29/50)
43. "Outlaw of the Plains" (7/6/50)
44. "White Man's Magic" (7/13/50)
45. "Trouble for Tonto" (7/20/50)
46. "Sheriff of Gunstock" (7/27/50)
47. "The Wrong Man" (8/3/50)
48. "The Beeler Gang" (8/10/50)
49. "The Star Witness" (8/17/50)
50. "The Black Widow" (8/24/50)
51. "The Whimsical Bandit" (8/31/50)
52. "Double Jeopardy" (9/7/50)

SEASON TWO

53. "Million Dollar Wallpaper" (9/14/50)
54. "Mission Bells" (9/21/50)
55. "Dead Man's Chest" (9/28/50)
56. "Outlaw's Revenge" (10/5/51)
57. "Danger Ahead" (10/12/50)
58. "Crime in Time" (10/19/50)
59. "Drink of Water" (10/26/50)
60. "Thieves Money" (11/2/50)
61. "The Squire" (11/9/50)
62. "Masked Deputy" (11/16/50)
63. "Bankers Choice" (11/23/50)
64. "Desert Adventure" (11/30/50)
65. "Bad Medicine" (12/7/50)
66. "One Jump Ahead" (12/14/50)
67. "Lady Killer" (12/21/50)
68. "Paid in Full" (12/28/50)
69. "Letter of the Law" (1/4/51)

70. "The Silent Voice" (1/11/51)
71. "The Outcast" (1/18/51)
72. "Backtrail" (1/25/51)
73. "Behind the Law" (2/1/51)
74. "Trouble at Black Rock" (2/8/51)
75. "Two Gold Lockets" (2/15/51)
76. "The Hooded Men" (2/22/51)
77. "Friend in Need" (3/1/51)
78. "Mr. Trouble" (3/8/51)

SEASON THREE
Starring John Hart

79. "Outlaw's Son" (9/11/52)
80. "Outlaw Underground" (9/18/52)
81. "Special Edition" (9/25/52)
82. "Desperado at Large" (10/2/52)
83. "Through the Wall" (10/9/52)
84. "Jeb's Gold Mine" (10/16/52)
85. "Frame for Two" (10/23/52)
86. "Ranger in Danger" (10/30/52)
87. "Delayed Action" (11/2/52)
88. "The Map" (11/13/52)
89. "Trial by Fire" (11/20/52)
90. "The Pledge" (11/27/52)
91. "Treason at Dry Creek" (12/4/52)
92. "The Condemned Man" (12/11/52)
93. "The New Neighbor" (12/18/52)
94. "Best Laid PLans" (12/25/52)
95. "Indian Charlie" (1/1/53)
96. "Empty Strong Box" (1/8/53)
97. "Trader Boggs" (1/15/53)
98. "Bandits in Uniform" (1/22/53)
99. "The Godless Men" (1/29/53)
100. "The Devil's Bog" (2/5/53)
101. "Right to Vote" (2/15/53)
102. "The Sheriff's Son" (2/19/53)
103. "Tumblerock Law" (2/26/53)
104. "Sinner by Proxy" (3/5/53)
105. "A Stage for Mademoiselle" (3/12/53)

106. "A Son by Adoption" (3/19/53)
107. "Mrs. Banker" (3/26/53)
108. "Trouble in Town" (4/2/53)
109. "Black Gold" (4/9/53)
110. "The Durango Kid" (4/16/53)
111. "The Deserter" (4/23/53)
112. "Embezzler's Harvest" (4/30/53)
113. "El Toro" (5/7/53)
114. "The Brown Pony" (5/14/53)
115. "Triple Cross" (5/21/53)
116. "Wake of War" (5/28/53)
117. "Death in the Forest" (6/4/53)
118. "Gentleman from Julesburg" (6/11/53)
119. "Hidden Fortune" (6/18/53)
120. "The Old Cowboy" (6/25/53)
121. "Woman from Omaha" (7/2/53)
122. "Gunpowder Joe" (7/9/53)
123. "The Midnight Rider" (7/16/53)
124. "Stage to Estacado" (7/23/53)
125. "The Perfect Crime" (7/30/53)
126. "The Ghost of Coyote Canyon" (8/6/53)
127. "Old Bailey" (8/13/53)
128. "Prisoner in Jeopardy" (8/20/53)
129. "Diamond in the Rough" (8/27/53)
130. "The Red Mark" (9/3/53)

SEASON FOUR
Clayton Moore Returns

131. "The Fugitive" (9/9/54)
132. "Ex-Marshal" (9/16/54)
133. "Message to Fort Apache" (9/23/54)
134. "The Frightened Woman" (9/30/54)
135. "Gold Town" (10/7/54)
136. "Six Gun Sanctuary" (10/14/54)
137. "Outlaw's Trail" (10/21/54)
138. "Stage to Teshimingo" (10/28/54)
139. "Texas Draw" (11/4/54)
140. "Rendezvous at Whipsaw" (11/11/54)
141. "Dan Reid's Fight for Life" (11/18/54)

142. "Tenderfoot" (11/25/54)
143. "A Broken Match" (12/2/54)
144. "Colorado Gold" (12/9/54)
145. "Homer with a High Hat" (12/16/54)
146. "Two for Juan Ringo" (12/23/54)
147. "The Globe" (12/30/54)
148. "Dan Reid's Sacrifice" (1/6/55)
149. "Enfield Rifle" (1/13/55)
150. "The School Story" (1/20/55)
151. "The Quiet Highwayman" (1/27/55)
152. "The Heritage of Treason" (2/3/55)
153. "The Lost Chalice" (2/10/55)
154. "Code of the Pioneers" (2/17/55)
155. "The Law Lady" (2/24/55)
156. "Uncle Ed" (3/3/55)
157. "Jornado Del Muerto" (3/10/55)
158. "Sunstroke Mesa" (3/17/55)
159. "Sawtelle Saga's End" (3/24/55)
160. "The Too-Perfect Signature" (3/31/55)
161. "Trigger Finger" (4/7/55)
162. "The Tell-Tale Bullet" (4/14/55)
163. "False Accusations" (4/28/55)
164. "Gold Freight" (5/5/55)
165. "Wanted: The Lone Ranger" (5/12/55)
166. "The Woman in the White Mask" (5/19/55)
167. "The Bounty Hunter" (5/26/55)
168. "Showdown at Sand Creek" (6/2/55)
169. "Heart of a Chester" (6/9/55)
170. "The Swami" (6/16/55)
171. "Sheriff for Sale" (6/23/55)
172. "Six-Gun Artist" (6/30/55)
173. "Death Goes to Press" (7/7/55)
174. "Return of Dice Dawson" (7/14/55)
175. "Adventure at Arbuckle" (7/21/55)
176. "The Return" (7/28/55)
177. "Framed for Murder" (8/4/55)
178. "Trapped" (8/11/55)
179. "The Bait: Gold" (8/18/55)
180. "The Sheriff's Wife" (8/25/55)

181. "Counterfeit Redskins" (9/1/55)
182. "One Nation Indivisible" (9/8/55)

SEASON FIVE
All Episodes Filmed in Color

183. "Wooden Rifle" (9/13/56)
184. "The Sheriff of Smoke Tree" (9/20/56)
185. "Counterfeit Mask" (9/27/56)
186. "No Handicap" (10/4/56)
187. "The Cross of Santo Domingo" (10/11/56)
188. "White Hawk's Decision" (10/18/56)
189. "The Return of Don Pedro O'Sullivan" (10/25/56)
190. "Quicksand" (11/1/56)
191. "Quarterhorse War" (11/8/56)
192. "The Letter Bride" (11/15/56)
193. "Hot Spell in Panamint" (11/22/56)
194. "The Twisted Track" (11/29/56)
195. "Decision for Chris McKeever" (12/6/56)
196. "Trouble at Tylerville" (12/13/56)
197. "Christmas Story" (12/20/56)
198. "Ghost Canyon" (12/27/56)
199. "Outlaw Masquerade" (1/3/57)
200. "The Avenger" (1/10/57)
201. "The Courage of Tonto" (1/17/57)
202. "The Breaking Point" (1/24/57)
203. "A Harp for Hannah" (1/31/57)
204. "A Message from Abe" (2/7/57)
205. "Code of Honor" (2/14/57)
206. "The Turning Point" (2/21/57)
207. "Dead Eye" (2/28/57)
208. "Clover in the Dust" (3/7/57)
209. "Slim's Boy" (3/14/57)
210. "Two Against Two" (3/21/57)
211. "Ghost Town Fury" (3/28/57)
212. "The Prince of Buffalo Gap" (4/4/57)
213. "The Law and Miss Aggie" (4/11/47)
214. "The Tarnished Star" (4/18/57)
215. "Canuck" (4/25/57)
216. "Mission for Tonto" (5/2/57)

217. "Journey to San Carlos" (5/9/57)
218. "The Banker's Son" (5/16/57)
219. "The Angel and the Outlaw" (5/23/57)
220. "Blind Witness" (5/30/57)
221. "Outlaws in Greasepaint" (6/6/57)

Guest-Starring Television Appearances

The Range Rider (1951)
Wild Bill Hickock (1952)
Hopalong Cassidy (1952)
The Gene Autry Show (1953)
Annie Oakley (1954)
The Gene Autry Show (1955)
Lassie (1959)

A Lone Ranger Chronology

1933   First radio broadcast of *The Lone Ranger* from WXYZ, Chicago, February 2.

1938   *The Lone Ranger* comic strip debuts on September 11.

1938   The fifteen-chapter Republic Pictures serial, *The Lone Ranger*, is released. It stars Lee Powell as the ranger and Chief Thundercloud as Tonto.

1939   *The Lone Ranger Rides Again*, another fifteen-chapter serial, is released by Republic. This one stars Bob Livingston and Chief Thundercloud.

1941   Earle Graser, the star of radio's *The Lone Ranger*, dies in an automobile accident on April 8. The role is assumed by Brace Beemer.

1949   First episode of *The Lone Ranger*, "Enter The Lone Ranger," airs on ABC-TV, September 15. It stars Clayton Moore and Jay Silverheels.

1952   John Hart replaces Clayton Moore as the Lone Ranger.

1954   Clayton Moore returns to *The Lone Ranger*.

1954   The final live broadcast of *The Lone Ranger* on radio, September 3.

1954   Jack Wrather buys all rights to the Lone Ranger from George W. Trendle.

1954   The feature film *The Lone Ranger* is released, starring Clayton Moore and Jay Silverheels.

1957   The final original *Lone Ranger* episode,"Outlaws in Greasepaint," airs June 6.The show will continue on the network in reruns until 1961.

1957   John Todd, radio's Tonto, dies at the age of eighty on July 14.

1958   The feature film *The Lone Ranger and the Lost City of Gold*, also starring Moore and Silverheels, is released.

1962   Fran Striker, the original *Lone Ranger* writer, dies in an automobile accident in September.

1965   Brace Beemer, the radio's longest-running Lone Ranger, dies at age sixty-two on March 1.

1966   A CBS-TV cartoon version of *The Lone Ranger* debuts, featuring the voices of Michael Rye and Sheperd Menken.

1972   George Washington Trendle, creator of *The Lone Ranger*, dies at age eighty-seven in May.

1979   The Wrather Corporation places a restraining order on Clayton Moore, forbidding him to appear in public in the character of the Lone Ranger.

1979   George Seaton, the first voice of the Lone Ranger on the radio, dies at age sixty-eight on June 28.

1980   Jay Silverheels dies March 5.
        The Tarzan/Lone Ranger Adventure Hour, another animated series, debuts on CBS-TV, September 13.

1981   The feature film *The Legend of the Lone Ranger* is released. It stars Klinton Spilsbury and Michael Horse.

1985   The Wrather Corporation's restraining order is lifted, allowing Clayton Moore to once again wear the mask of the Lone Ranger.

Suggested Further Reading

Felbinger, Lee J. *Lone Ranger Pictorial Scrapbook*. Green Lane PA: Countryside Advertising, 1989.

Holland, Dave. *From Out of the Past: A Pictorial History of the Lone Ranger*. Granada Hills CA: The Holland House, 1989.

Rothel, David. *Who Was That Masked Man? The Story of the Lone Ranger*. South Brunswick & New York: A. S. Barnes and Company, 1976.

Van Hise, James. *Who Was That Masked Man? The Story of the Lone Ranger*. Las Vegas: Pioneer Books, 1990.

Index

A

ABC–TV, 199, 256
Academy Awards, 5
Acuna, Frank, 118
Adelson, Lenny, 182
Adventures of Frank and Jesse James (film serial), 104, 248
African Americans, 18–19, 137
Al and Connie Seaman Agency, 38, 39
Aldridge, Kay, 63
Allen, Jack, 68
Allen, Sally. *See* Moore, Sally Allen (2nd wife)
Allied Powers, 71
Along the Oregon Trail (film), 103, 244
Alpha Sigma Lambda (fraternity), 29
American Broadcasting Company, 199, 256
American Indians. *See* Native Americans
American Society for the Prevention of Cruelty to Animals, 108
Amos 'n' Andy (radio serial), 112
Anderson, Robert B., 232
Andrews, Dana, 54
Anita (Clarita's sister), 218
Appaloosa Andy (TV serial), 232
Apple Valley, 122
Aqua Velva commercials, 199–200
Army Air Force, 71–76
Arnaz, Desi, 155

Arness, Jim, 128
Art Institute of Chicago, 30
Asheville (N.C.), 161–62
ASPCA, 108
Autry, Gene
  cheering for, x
  in *The Cowboy and the Indians*, 117
  Lone Ranger role and, 7
  movie set of, 238–39
  ranch of, 158
  Republic and, 6, 62
  Selander and, 181

B

Bachelor's Daughter, The (film), 244
Bachrach, Bill, 30
Ball, Lucille, 155
Bandits of Corsica, The (film), 247
Bandits of Eldorado (film), 245
Banner (horse), 65, 99
Barbed Wire (film), 246
Barcroft, Roy
  in *The Ghost of Zorro*, 105
  in *The Lone Ranger* TV serial, 156
  E. Parker and, 102
  in *Radar Men from the Moon*, 132
  Woods and, 100–101
Barcroft, Vera, 100
Bari, Lynn, 54
Barry, Gene, 199
Barrymore, John, 68, 69
Baxter, Les, 182
BBC, 158, 185, 186
Beau Geste (film), 101

Bedford, Duke of, 187
Beemer, Brace, xii, 1
  aging fans of, 236
  Bletcher and, 8
  death of, 256
  public appearances of, 6, 9–10
  vocal quality of, 9, 112, 118
Beery, Wallace, 49
Behr, Johnny
  offer by, 36, 37
  rigging of, 32, 139
  training by, 30–31
Belfast (N. Ireland), 189
Bellamy, Earl, 146–47
Belmont Plaza Hotel (New York), 41
Benedict, Billy, 62
Bennett, Joan, 58
Bennet, Spencer Gordon, 134, 138, 140
Benny, Jack, 5, 196
Bergman, Al, 29
Berle, Milton, 196
Bettger, Lyle, 159
Beverly Hills, 74, 212
Beverly Hills Hotel, 151–52
"Beyond the Blue Horizon" (song), 3, 4
Big Bear (Calif.), 138, 140
Bissel, Whit, 156
Black Book, The (film serial), 134
Black Dakotas, The (film), 247
Black Dragons, The (film), 69, 70, 244
Blake, Pamela, 105
Blazing the Overland Trail

(film serial), 134
Bletcher, Billy, 7, 8
Blue Bowl (diner), 41
Bogart, Humphrey, 47
Bold Caballero, The (film),
105
Bond, Ward, 54
Booth, Adrian (Lorna Gray),
62, 63, 103
Bowery Boys, 56
Boxer, Joel, 207
Boy Scouts, 25
Boyd Martin Bullet (boat),
23–24
Boyer, Charles, 57
Bradna, Fred, 50
Bradna, Olympe, 50
Brannon, Freddy
The Crimson Ghost and,
80
G-Men Never Forget and,
101, 102
The Ghost of Zorro and,
105, 106
on KPM plaque, 162, 179
Radar Men from the Moon
and, 132, 134
Brennan, Walter, 198
Brent, George, 58
Brigham Young,
Frontiersman (film), 138
Britain, 158, 185–89, 191
British Broadcasting
Corporation, 158, 185,
186
Broken Arrow (film), 144
Bronson Canyon, 121, 159
Brooks, Rand, 45, 155, 210
Brown, Joe E., 144
Buchanan, Edgar, 135
Buck (horse), 179
Buffalo Bill in Tomahawk
Territory (film), 137–38,
246
Bugliosi, Vincent, 228*n*
Bullitt (film), 11
Bullocks Wilshire (firm),
192
Burns, Lillian, 49
Butterworth, Ethel, 50
Buttrum, Pat, 199

C
Caesar, Sid, 196
California, 21, 192–93, 194,
212
Canada, 22–24, 158
Canoga Park (Calif.), 148
Canova, Judy, 50
Canutt, Yakima, 101–2
Capone, Al, 26, 27, 101
Capone, Bobby, 27
Capra, Frank, 44–45
Captain from Castille (film),
117
Captive of Billy the Kid
(film), 246
Cardiff (Wales), 185
Carey, Harry ("Dobie"), Jr.,
156
Carey, Harry, Sr., 16
Carroll, John, 50
Carson (Calif.), 212
Cassidy, Hopalong, 116, 134,
181, 196
CBS Television Center
(Studio City), 62
CBS TV, 256–57
Chandler, Lane, 159
Charleston (S.C.), 162
Charley's Aunt (film), 5
Chertok, Jack
casting by, 113–15, 116, 117
cost cutting by, 121–22
production by, 128
Chicago
auto trips from, 23
childhood in, 24–34
funeral in, 75
modeling in, 37–38
race riot in, 18–19
Chicago World's Fair (1934),
32–34, 37, 139
Children's Home Society,
190, 191
Chinese Theater
(Hollywood), 240
Christina (maid), 18, 19
Christine, Virginia, 156
Ciro's (nightclub), 51, 69
Cisco Kid, The (TV serial),
157
Citizen Kane (film), 62

Cliffhangers, The (TV
special), 101
Coates, Phyllis, 104, 136, 140
Coconut Grove (nightclub),
51
Coffin, Tristram, 66, 132, 155
Cohan, George M., 17
Colbert, Claudette, 45
Colt revolvers, 225–26
Columbia Broadcasting
System, 256–57
Columbia Pictures, Inc.,
43–46
Compton, Johnny, 100
Connors, Chuck, 155, 199
Connover, Harry, 40
Conrad, Robert, 239
Cooper, Gary, 53, 210
Corning Ware commercials,
201
Corrigan, Ray ("Crash"), 8
Corriganville (Calif.), 158
Corsican Brothers, The
(film), 58
Count of Monte Cristo, The
(film), 58
Country Girl, The (film), 5
Courtney, Chuck, 128, 227
Covered Wagon Days (radio
serial), 3
Cowboy and the Indians, The
(film), 117, 245
Cowboy from Brooklyn, The
(film), 47, 243
Crime School (film), 47, 243
Crimson Ghost, The (film
serial), 80–81, 82, 247
Culver City (Calif.), 75, 123
Curcio, Amedeo, 218
Curcio, Rose, 218
Curtis, Alan, 38–39
Cyclone Fury (film), 245
Cyclotrode "X" [*Crimson*
Ghost] (film), 80–81, 82,
247

D
Dale (dog), 75, 76
Darkest Africa (film serial),
79, 134
Darrell, Steve, 104

Daughters of Atrias (play), 48

Day, Laraine, 49

Day at the Races, A (film), 5

Daytona Beach High School, 35–36, 37

Dead End Kids, 47, 56

Deeds, Jack, 5–6, 112

Dees, Rick, 239, 240

Des Plaines (Ill.), 20

Desert Passage (film), 246

Detroit, 23, 32, 111, 112

Devon Theater (Chicago), 16

Dick Tracy (film), 6

Dienell Spring Water (firm), 25

Disney, Walt, 7, 157

Disneyland Hotel (Anaheim), 153

Dix, Richard, 182

Dodge commercials, 200

Dolores (roommate), 74

Dorn, Art
   in court, 208–9
   letter to, 216
   negotiations by, 215
   on petitions, 212
   on rights, 209–10
   Stunnel and, 204–6

Douglas Air Force Base, 73

Down Laredo Way (film), 246

Dr. Bernardo's Hospital, 187

Dracula (film), 69

Drake Hotel (Chicago), 30

Dunne, Irene, 44

Durango Kid, 138

E

Eastern Square (wrestling finals), 144

Ed Sullivan Show, The (TV serial), 196–98

Edgewater Beach Hotel (Chicago), 29

Edinburgh, 187

Edlebute, Graham, 189

Edward Small Productions, 49

El Dorado Pass (film), 106, 138–39, 244

Elam, Jack, 128

Elizabeth the Queen (play), 5

Ellerbrook, Frank, 73, 74

Encino (Calif.), 192, 211

English, John, 7

Erie (Pa.), 32

Evans, Dale, x

F

Fairbanks, Douglas, 105

Fairhaven (Mass.), 217

Fang (dog), 67

Far Frontier, The (film), 245

Farmer, Frances, 50

Farnsworth, Richard, 33

Farnsworth, Mrs. Richard, 33

Fisher, Theresa Violet. *See* Moore, Theresa Violet Fisher (mother)

Fleishman, Doc, 45, 46

Flying Behrs (trapeze troupe)
   experience with, 112, 114
   formation of, 31
   hobby status of, 35
   rigging of, 32, 139
   tour by, 36, 37
   at World's Fair, 32–34

Fond Du Lac (Wis.), 20

Ford, Gerald R., 228*n*

Ford, Glenn, 199

Ford, John, 102, 156

Forte, Joe, 81

Foster, Vernon, 209

Foy, Brian, 46–47

Foy, Fred, 4, 10, 12

Fraker, William A., 11–12

Francis, Arlene, 198

Francis, Mary, 56–58

Freberg, Stan, 147–48

Fresno Police Department, 235

Friewald, Eric, 181

Froelich, Fred, 125, 126

From Out of the Past (Holland), 4

Fromme, Lynette Alice ("Squeaky"), 228*n*

G

G-Men Never Forget (film serial), 101–2, 248

Gable, Clark, 45

Garden of the Gods (rock grouping), 121

Gay Amigo, The (film), 245

Gene Autry Western Heritage Award, 238

General Mills, Inc., 120, 200

General Service Studios, 155, 156

Geno's Pizza commercials, 147–48, 199

Gentry, Curt, 228*n*

Georgie (monkey), 67

German Americans, 18

Germany, 69, 71

Geronimo, Chief, 144

Ghost of Zorro, The (film serial), 104–7, 109, 113, 248

Gifford, Frances, 63

Glenwood Middies (gang), 26

Go Chase Yourself (film), 243

Goldbeck, Willis, 159

Golden Boot Awards, x, 238

Golden Gloves (boxing championship), 144

Goldwyn, Sam, 49

Good Ship Anne, 145

Gordon, Bob, 198

Grady, Billy, 47, 48-49

Granada Theater (Chicago), 99

Grant, Cary, xii

Granville, Bonita. *See* Wrather, Bonita Granville

Graser, Earle, 6
   death of, 9, 112, 256
   popularity of, 8

Gray, Lorna (Adrian Booth), 62, 63, 103

Great Britain, 158, 185–89, 191

Great Depression, 80

Greatest American Hero, The (TV serial), 234

Gunfighters of the Northwest (film serial), 138, 139–41, 248
Gunsmoke (TV serial), 128, 239

H

Hal Roach Studios, 123, 124, 155
Hale, Monte, 103
Hall, Andy, 56
Hall, Huntz, 56
Hall, Jon, 49, 53
Hall, Thurston, 62–63
Hank and Honey (radio serial), 2
Happy Days (TV serial), 128, 234
Hardy, Oliver, 123
Hardy, Phil, 11
Hart, John, 10, 180, 251–52, 256
  competence of, 131–32
  fan rejection of, 151
  final episode of, 141
  in *Gunfighters of the Northwest*, 140–41
  horse of, 156
  in *The Legend of the Lone Ranger*, 12
  masking of, 153
  Trendle silence on, 152
  in *Vanity Fair*, 199
Hart, William S., 16, 28, 99
Harvey Girls, The (film), 49
Hawk of Wild River (film), 246
Hayden, Gay, 40
Hayden, Russell, 134, 181–82
Hayt Grammar School (Chicago), 27, 29
Hayward, Louis, 58
Hayward, Susan, 47
Heathrow Airport (London), 185
Heisler, Stuart, 159, 160
Heldorado (film), 244
Hello Annapolis (film), 244
Helter Skelter (Bugliosi and Gentry), 228*n*
Hendlmyer, Jack, 226

Henning, Ira, 20
Hi Yo Silver (film), 11
"Hi Yo Silver" (song), 182
Hibbs, Gene, 127
Hightower, Emma, 19
Hoibe, Jim, 227
Holland, Dave, 2, 4, 8
Hollywood
  early career in, 43–59
  glamour in, 69
  move from, 193
  preparation for, 38
  social connections in, 68
  Velez appearances in, 51–52
  in wartime, 74, 75
Hollywood Canteen, 74
Hollywood Chamber of Commerce, 237
Hollywood Walk of Fame, 148, 239–40
Holt, Tim, 103, 181
Hooker, Hugh, 117
Hooper (film), 200
Hopalong Cassidy (TV serial), 196
Horse, Michael, 257
Horton, Robert, 199
Houston (Tex.), 225–26
Houston Police Department, 226
How the West Was Won (film), 160
Hudkins, Ace, 99, 100
Hudkins, Ode, 99, 100
Hughes, Howard, 153
Humphries, Pat, 223–24

I

Illinois Athletic Club, 29–32, 192
Indian Actors Workshop, 145
Indians. *See* Native Americans
International Lady (film), 58, 244
Iowa University, 139
It Happened One Night (film), 44–45
Iverson's Ranch, 13, 227

The Crimson Ghost shot at, 81
Jungle Drums of Africa shot at, 136
The Lone Ranger TV serial shot at, 121–22, 146, 158
The Perils of Nyoka shot at, 66
Radar Men from the Moon shot at, 133

J

James, Frank, 104
James, Jesse, 82, 99, 104
Japan, 69, 71
Jesse James Rides Again (film serial), xii
  cast of, 247–48
  production of, 99–100
  Stirling in, 101
  wagon stunt in, 82
Jewell, Jim, 3, 9
Jolly, Stan, 81
Jolson, Al, 191
Jones, Buck, 3, 181
Jones, Jennifer, 5
Judge Roy Bean (TV serial), 135
Jungle Drums of Africa (film serial), 104, 135–37, 138, 248
Jungle Girl (film), 63
Justice of the West (film), 247

K

Kanab (Utah), 158, 160–61
Kangawoowoo (TV serial), 198
Kansas Pacific (film), 246–47
Katt, William, 232
KCET (PBS station), 153
Kelly, DeForest, 128
Kennedy, Douglas, 181
Kennedy, John F., 237
Key Largo (film), 117
KIIS-FM (radio station), 239
King of the Carnival (film serial), 79

King of the Rocket Men
(film), 134
Kingman (Ariz.), 73, 74
Kit Carson (film)
cast of, 53–54, 244
director of, 53, 106, 125
fight scene in, 106
hair style for, 52, 54
premiere of, 57
roles subsequent to, 58
shooting delay in, 55
Kyser, Kay, 73

L
La Conga (nightclub), 50
Ladies' Home Journal, The,
28
Lake Michigan, 30
Lake Tahoe, 194
Lake Zurich, 20
Landis, Carole, 47
Lane, Priscilla, 47
LaShelle, Art, 50–51
Lassie (dog), 161
Lassie (TV serial), 153, 161,
203
Lauder, Harry, 128
Laughlin (Nev.), 218
Laurel, Stan, 123
Lawdell, Larry, 33
Lebovitz, Annie, 199
Lee, Rowland V., 58
Legend of the Lone Ranger,
The (film), xii, xiii,
11–12
box-office failure of, xiv,
215–16
casting of, 12, 210, 234
content of, 207
preproduction of, 206
release of, 257
Lincolnwood (Ill.), 224–25
Lindbergh, Charles, Jr., 66
Little, Boyd, 33
"Liver Lip" (horse), 117, 156,
159
Livingston, Monty, 197, 198
Livingston, Robert, 1, 7–8,
105, 256
Loggia, Robert, 199
London (England), 187–88

Lone Pine (Calif.), 158
Lone Ranger, The (animated
cartoon), 256–57
Lone Ranger, The (comic
strip), 111, 158, 256
Lone Ranger, The (film feature), 11, 180
cast of, 247
Granville in, 154
production of, 159–61
release of, 256
Lone Ranger, The (film serial), 6–7, 11, 112, 256
Lone Ranger, The (radio
serial)
aging fans of, 236
Beemer in, 9–10
behavior code for, 14
Bletcher and, 8
early stars of, 5–6, 112
final episode of, 256
first episode of, 4, 256
planning for, 2–4, 111
stations carrying, 158
Tonto role in, 143
Lone Ranger, The (TV
serial), xii, 203, 249–55
Beemer and, 9, 10
behavior code for, 15–16
in Britain, 185
casting for, 113–17
character roles in, 107,
153
dialogue in, 125–27,
145–46, 154
distancing from, 135
final episode of, 180, 256
firing from, 131–32
first episode of, 66, 121,
256
Graser recording in, 6
guns in, 222, 224
horse stunts in, 65, 99, 107,
157
identity concealed in, 8
kissing in, 226
personal identification
with, 232–33, 240–41
production of, 116–28,
195–96
props in, 162

public appearances for,
14
radio parallel to, 10
recent fans of, 236–37
repackaging of, 182, 247
return to, 141, 151–53
Seitz Jr. and, 53
title sequence of, 13
in Wrather era, 152–58,
232
mentioned, 144, 147, 199,
227
Lone Ranger and the Lost
City of Gold, The (film
feature), 11, 180–83,
203, 233
actress in, 55
cast of, 247
release of, 185, 196, 256
"Lone Ranger Creed, The"
(Striker), 129–30
Lone Ranger Peace Patrol,
198, 232
Lone Ranger Rides Again,
The (film serial), 7–8,
11, 256
Lone Ranger Rock, 13, 15
Long Beach (Calif.), 153
Loon Lake, 22–24
Lord, Marjorie, 128
Los Angeles
early career in, 43
living costs in, 193
return to, 189–90
social problems in, 194
wedding in, 218
Lowry, Bob, 50
Lucky Strike cigarettes, 23
Lugosi, Bela, 69
Lydecker, Howard, 134
Lydecker, Theodore, 134
Lynn, Jeffrey, 47

M
Ma and Pa Kettle (film
serial), 62
McCoy, Charlie, 25
MacIntosh (clothier), 101
Macombo (nightclub), 51
McQuarrie, Earl, 151–52
Madison Square Garden

(New York), 144
Mahoney, Jock, 138–39, 140,
 199
Malibu Canyon Road, 81
Maltin, Leonard, 101
Manhunters (radio serial), 2
Manson, Charles, 228
Marshall, George, 56
Marshall of Amarillo (film),
 244
Martin, Richard, 103
Marx Brothers, 5
Mask of Zorro, The (film),
 105
Masked Raiders (film), 103,
 245
Massey, Ilona, 58
Matthews, Sven, 31
Maynard, Ken, 16
Meadow, Herb, 159
Melody Ranch, 158, 236–37
Menken, Sheperd, 255
Mergatroyd (horse), 179
Metro-Goldwyn-Mayer, Inc.,
 xii
 casting by, 47
 Chertok and, 114
 screen tests for, 48–49
 theater chains of, 61
Michaels, Bob, 208, 209, 215
Miljan, John, 181
Minneapolis
 family visit in, 127
 personal appearance in,
  200
 residence in, 193–94
 robbery in, 219–20
 TV appearance in, 198
Miracle on 34th Street
 (film), 5
Mix, Tom, 16, 99
Monogram Studios, 66, 70
Monroe, Marilyn, 124
Montana Territory (film), 246
Montclair Hotel (New York),
 41
Monte Walsh (film), 11
Montgomery, Douglas, 50
Montoya, Henry, 31
Moore, Clarita Petrone
 (fourth wife), 218

Moore, Connie (third wife),
 217–18, 223
Moore, Dawn Angela
 (daughter), 190–92
 in Hollywood, 239–40
 in Lake Tahoe, 194
 in Los Angeles, 218
 in Minneapolis, 193, 221
 on Spahn Ranch, 227
Moore, Howard (brother),
 18, 28–29
 fishing trips of, 20
 at Loon Lake, 24
 race riot and, 19
 shooting by, 21
 trapeze work of, 31
 in Tuba City, 54
Moore, Mary Francis (first
 wife), 56–58
Moore, Sally Allen (second
 wife)
 Barcrofts and, 100
 celebration with, 115, 240
 collecting by, 162, 179
 Dawn and, 190–91, 192
 death of, 217
 first TV episode and, 121
 illness of, 208
 introduction to, 68
 in Minneapolis, 127, 193,
  221
 Petrones and, 218
 in Santa Monica, 76
 serials production and,
  135
 on Silverheels, 148
 in Tarzana, 139
 vocal exercises and, 118
 in wartime, 71, 73–75
Moore, Sprague (brother)
 girls and, 29
 last visit with, 75
 modeling by, 37–38
 office of, 27
 race riot and, 18–19
 shooting by, 21
Moore, Sprague C. (father)
 death of, 75
 favorite radio shows of,
  112
 horse given by, 25

 at Loon Lake, 22–23
 medical aspirations and,
  35–36
 New York sojourn and, 39,
  41
 office of, 27, 38
 race riot and, 18–19
 shipboard visit of, 54, 55
 sports activities of, 20–21
 in Tuba City, 54
 tuition paid by, 45
 winter activities of, 24
 wound bandaged by,
  21–22
Moore, Theresa Violet Fisher
 (mother), 18, 20
 at Canadian border, 23
 childhood friend of, 43
 at Loon Lake, 22, 24
 New York sojourn and,
  39
 race riot and, 19
 telegram to, 41
 trips by, 21
 in Tuba City, 54
Morgan, Bob, 160
Motion Picture and
 Television Home and
 Hospital, 148
MTV, 120
Mutiny (film), 245

N
Nash, Noreen, 181
National Cowboy Hall of
 Fame, 238
National Lacrosse Team
 (Canada), 144
Native Americans
 culture of, 147
 in films, 145
 in *Kit Carson*, 106
 pride of, 231
 struggles of, 235
 in Wisconsin, 21, 22
 See also Six Nations
Nazarro, Ray, 138, 139
Neal, Tom
 S. Allen and, 68
 auditioning by, 42
 Chertok and, 114

friendship with, 40–41, 75, 210
in *Jungle Girl*, 63
night life of, 50
party hosted by, 67
screen test by, 48–49
Neberroth, Harold, 38–39
Needham, Hal, 200
Neill, Noel, 104
Nell (bear), 25
New York City, 35–42, 44
Newhall Walk of Fame, 238–39
Nibley, Sloan, 101
Nigh, William, 70
Night Stage to Galveston (film), 246
Nixon, Julie, 232
Nixon, Richard M., 186, 232
Nixon, Tricia, 232
Notre Dame (South Bend prep school), 27
Nyoka and the Tigermen. See *Perils of Nyoka, The* (film serial)

O

O'Brian, Hugh, 199
O'Brien, George, 16
O'Brien, Pat, 47
O'Keefe, Dennis, 50
Old Tucson (Ariz.), 155
Olympic Auditorium (Los Angeles), 52
Omnibus (TV serial), 196
One Flew Over the Cuckoo's Nest (film), 11
Oregon Trail, 54
Orsati, Al, 49
Orsati, Frank, 48
Osborn, Bud, 135
Othello (play), 180
Our Gang (film serial), 123
Ouspenskaya, Maria, 48
"Outlaws in Greasepaint" (TV episode), 180, 255
Outlaws of Pine Ridge (film), 244

P

Painted Stallion, The (film), 6

Palm Desert (Calif.), 218
Palos Park (Chicago), 24, 25
Pangras, Phil, 193
Paramount Pictures Corporation, 61
Park Lane Trailer Park, 74–75
Parker, Eddie, 102
Parker, Fess, 199
Parsons, Louella, 52–53, 68
Peach, Kenneth, 182
Pearl, Minnie, 198
Peoria (Ill.), 200
Perick, Robert, 56
Perils of Nyoka, The (film serial), 63–67, 79
cast of, 247
The Crimson Ghost and, 80
Jesse James Rides Again and, 99
The Lone Ranger TV serial and, 157
vocal quality in, 118
Perils of Pauline (film serial), 101
Petrone, Clarita, 218
Pickens, Slim, 156
Pinson, Alan, 123
Pioneer Town (Calif.), 134
Pirate's Den (nightclub), 69
Plainsman, The (film), 101
Playhouse 90 (TV serial), 196
Plunderers, The (film), 244
Powell, Dick, 47
Powell, Lee, 1, 7, 8, 255
Powers, John Robert, 39–40, 41
Powers Agency, 40, 41–42
Priest, Ivy Baker, 232
Princess Margaret Rose Hospital (Edinburgh), 187
Private Secretary (TV serial), 155
Purcell, Sarah, 215
Purple Monster Strikes, The (film), 134
Pyle, Denver, 128

Q

Queen Mary (ship), 153
Queenie (dog), 68
Quigley, Charles, 80

R

Radar Men from the Moon (film serial), 132–33, 134, 248
Radio Hams (film), 243
Raiders, The (film), 246
Raiders of the Lost Ark (film), 67
Rand, Sally, 33–34
Randall, Glenn, 180
Range Rider, The (TV serial), 139
Ranger Realty, 193
Rathbone, Basil, 58
Ratoff, Gregory, 58–59
Reading (Pa.), 180
Real People (TV serial), 214–15
Reap the Wild Wind (film), 101
Reeves, George, 104, 136
Remington firearm, 224–25
Republic Cave, 81–82, 133
Republic Studios, 61–70, 79–109, 146, 151
casting director of, 59
fight scenes for, 105–6, 122
The Ghost of Zorro, 104–7, 109, 113, 248
horse work for, 99–100, 157
The Lone Ranger, 6–7, 11, 112, 255
The Lone Ranger Rides Again, 7–8, 11, 255
postwar contacts with, 76
return to, 77, 132–40
mentioned, xii, 1, 75, 162
"Return of Dice Dawson" (TV episode), 156
"Return of Don Pedro O'Sullivan" (TV episode), 152–53
Riders of the Purple Sage (singing group), 161

Riders of the Whistling Pines
(film), 245
Rifkin, Joe, 43–46, 48
Rifleman, The (TV serial),
155
Ringling Brothers and
Barnum and Bailey
Show, 50
RKO Radio Pictures, Inc., 39
Roach Studios, 123, 124, 155
Robertson, Dale, 199
Rogers, Roy
cheering for, x
motorcycling by, 101
Randall and, 180
Republic and, 6, 62
Rohr (adoption agent), 191
Rosemary's Baby (film), 11
Ross, Marion, 128
Ross, Norman, Sr., 33
Rossini, Gioacchino, xi, 4,
111–12
Rothel, David, 5
Rowland, Henry, 136–37
Ryder, Red, 109
Rye, Michael, 255

S

Saint Gertrude's Catholic
Church (Chicago), 24
Saint Ignatious Church
(Chicago), 25–26
St. John's Hospital (Santa
Monica), 216
Sales, Soupy, 198
San Fernando Valley, 117
San Francisco, 236
Santa Ana, 76
Santa Anita, 69
Santa Monica, 76, 216
Saturday Evening Post, The,
28
Scandals (revue), 56
Schaefer, Robert, 181
Scottsdale (Ariz.), 21
Scout (horse), 146, 147
Seaman Agency, 38, 39
Sears, Roebuck and
Company, 38, 40
Seaton, George, 5, 112, 257
Seitz, George, Jr., 53, 125, 126

Seitz, George B., Sr., 53, 106,
125
Selander, Lesley, 181–82
Senn High School
(Chicago), 29
Sennett, Mack, 62
Sergeant Madden (film), 49,
243
*Sergeant Preston of the
Yukon* (TV serial), 153
Shakespeare, William, 152,
180, 189
Sharpe, Dave, 134
earnings of, 66
in *G-Men Never Forget*,
102–3
in *The Perils of Nyoka*,
64–65
riding lessons of, 157
Shay, Bill, 180
She Wore a Yellow Ribbon
(film), 101, 156
Sheppard Field (Tex.),
71–73
Sheriff of Wichita (film), 245
Sherrill, Lou, 113–14, 115
Shining Hour, The (play), 47
Short, Antrim, 113
Show Boat (film), 49
Sidney, George, 49
Silver (horse), 143, 147,
179–80
in commercials, 200
early concept of, 3
kissing of, 226
"Liver Lip" as, 117, 156, 159
proposed comedy
appearance of, 234
public appearances of,
157, 161–62
rearing by, 65
in title sequences, 13
weight of, 186
Silverheels, Jay, 11, 116–17,
143–49, 152, 255
in Apple Valley, 122
Beemer and, 10
in commercials, 199
death of, 148–49, 255
dialogue of, 126–27
greatness of, 231

J. Hart and, 132
heart attack of, 127
in Kanab, 160
in *The Lone Ranger and
the Lost City of Gold,*
181, 183
Monroe and, 124
public appearances by,
14, 147, 236
recovery of, 128
report to, 186
stunt doubles for, 123
in Tarzana, 139
in two-shot, 125, 126
Walk of Fame star for, 239
Silverheels, Mary, 148
Silver's Pride (horse), 10
Six Nations, 144–45
Six Nations Indian Reservation, 116, 143, 149
Small, Eddie
contract with, 49
Kit Carson and, 53–54, 55
name changed by, 17, 50
release by, 59
roles provided by, 58
Smith, Harold J. *See*
Silverheels, Jay
Smoky and the Bandit
(film), 200
*Snow White and the Seven
Dwarfs* (film), 7
Son of Geronimo (film seri-
al), 134–35, 248
Son of Monte Cristo, The
(film), 58, 244
Song of Bernadette, The
(film), 5
Sonora (Calif.), 158
Sothern, Ann, 127, 155
South Bend Bait Company,
20
South Carolina State Fire-
man's Association, 223
South Chicago, 24
South of Death Valley (film),
243
South of Pago Pago (film),
49, 50, 53, 58
Spahn, George, 226–28
Spartanburg (S.C.), 223–24

Index

Spielberg, Steven, 67
Spilsbury, Klinton, xii, 210, 255
Spruce Goose (airplane), 153
Stagecoach (film), 102
"Star Spangled Banner" (anthem), 17
Star Trek (TV serial), 128, 237
Starrett, Charles, 106, 138, 139
Steele, Tom, 64–65
  in *The Crimson Ghost*, 80
  in *The Ghost of Zorro*, 105–6
  hat trick of, 122
  in *Radar Men from the Moon*, 132, 133
  riding lessons of, 100, 157
  shooting lessons of, 21
  stunts by, 82, 134
Stengler, Mack, 119
Stenius, George (George Seaton), 5, 112, 255
Stirling, Linda, 80, 101
Stratford (England), 189
Streisand, Barbra, 191
Striker, Fran, 111
  death of, 255
  early contacts with, 2
  first scripts of, 3–4
  Graser death and, 9
  "The Lone Ranger Creed," 129–30
  TV casting by, 113–15, 116, 117
  vocal training by, 118
Studio City (Calif.), 62, 67
Stunnel, Stanley, 204, 205, 216
Stuntman's Hall of Fame, 236
Sullivan, Ed, 50, 196–98
Sullivan Junior High School (Chicago), 29
Superman (TV serial), 104, 136, 157

T

Taffy (dog), 57–58, 75, 76
Talbot, Lyle, 156
Tarzan/Lone Ranger Adventure Hour, The (animated cartoon), 255
Tarzana (Calif.), 139, 179
Tate, Sharon, 228
Terhune, Max, 8
Texas Rangers (baseball team), 214
Texas Rangers (military force), 212
  in *The Legend of the Lone Ranger*, 11, 207
  in *The Lone Ranger* film serial, 7
  in *The Lone Ranger* TV serial, 120
  Trendle concept of, 3, 111
Thames River, 187, 188
Thomas, Miles, 76
Three Godfathers (film), 156
Three Little Pigs, The (film), 7
Three Mesquiteers, 8
Three Rivers (Wis.), 20
Thundercloud, Chief, 7, 8, 255
Todd, John, 4, 255
Too Many Girls (film), 144
Topanga Canyon, 81, 133
Towne, Aline, 132
Trail of the Lonesome Pine, The (film), 138
Trendle, George Washington
  announcement approved by, 5
  authenticity desired by, 129
  Beemer and, 9–10
  Bletcher and, 8
  cost cutting by, 121–22
  death of, 255
  diction required by, 125, 154
  film versions and, 10–11, 158–59
  firing by, 130, 131
  moral standards of, 2–3, 4, 14
  original conception of, 111, 154–55
  recall by, 141, 151–52
  rights sold by, 153, 158, 255
  script change and, 126
  TV casting by, 113–15, 117, 149
  vocal quality desired by, 118
  WXYZ purchased by, 1–2
  Yates and, 6–7
Trocadero (nightclub), xii, 51
Troush, Robert, 31
Tuba City (Ariz.), 54
Tuxedo Junction (film), 62, 73, 242

U

United Artists Corporation, 137
United Service Organizations, Inc., 73
United States Army Air Force, 71–76
United States Savings Stamps, 232
Universal Pictures Company, 11
University of Iowa, 139
USO, 73

V

Valejo (Calif.), 212
Valley of the Sun (film), 144
Van Horn, Emil, 65–66
Van Sickel, Dale, 132
Vanity Fair (magazine), 199
Velez, Lupe, xii, 50–53, 56–57, 67
Vietnam, 234
Vigilantes Are Coming, The (film), 6
Vin, Bob, 31, 139

W

Walk of Fame. *See* Hollywood Walk of Fame; Newhall Walk of Fame

Walk the Proud Land (film), 144
Walker, Clint, 199
Wallace, George, 132, 133
"Wanted: The Lone Ranger" (TV episode), 180
Ward, Bill, 123, 124, 160
Warner Bros. Pictures, Inc., xii, 65
early work for, 46–48, 49
theater chains of, 61
Warner Bros. Studios (Burbank), 159
Warren (cousin), 48
Wasserman, Frieda, 19, 20, 22
Wayne, John
horse of, 65, 99
Republic and, 6, 62
serials of, 103
in *Stagecoach*, 102
"Three Mesquiteers" and, 8
Wayne Avenue Middies (gang), 26
Weaver, Dennis, 128, 239
Weissmuller, Johnny
Bachrach and, 30
Dawn and, 192
Parsons on, 52
swimming trunks of, 67
Velez and, 50–51
Weissmuller, Pete, 30
Welles, Orson, 62
Wells, Jacqueline, 44, 45
West Side (Chicago), 32
Western films, 237–38
Western Heritage Award, 238
What's My Line? (TV serial), 198
Whelan, Tim, 58
"When the West Was Fun" (TV show), 199
When Were You Born? (film), 47, 241
White, George, 56
White, Les, 46
Whiteman, Paul, 29
Wilcox, Rudy, 46
Wild, Wild West, The (TV serial), 239

Wilke, Bob, 159
William Tell Overture, xi, 4, 111–12, 115. 207
William the Conqueror, 188
Winkler, Henry, 234
Wisconsin, 20, 21–22
Witney, William, 7, 63–64, 67, 80, 182
Woburn Abbey (England), 187
Wong, Anna May, 47
Woodland Hills (Calif.), 148
Woods, Harry, 100–1
World War I, 18
World War II, 71–76, 80
World's Fair (1934), 32–34, 37, 139
Wrather, Bonita Granville, 154, 210
Lassie and, 161, 203
in *The Lone Ranger* feature, 159
restraining order lifted by, 216–17
Wrather, Jack, 11, 156
alienation from, 210–11
artistic consultation with, 154, 232
business negotiations with, 152
chance meeting with, 205
color filming by, 157
death of, 216
The Ed Sullivan Show and, 196, 197, 198
Edlebute and, 189
final gesture of, 217
informality with, 155
Lassie and, 153, 203
The Lone Ranger and the Lost City of Gold and, 180–81
The Lone Ranger feature and, 159, 161
rights sold to, 153, 158, 255
Stunnel and, 204
Wrather Corporation
complaints to, xiv
court ruling on, 209
demands by, 205, 206, 209–10, 211

fan protest of, 213–14
fees for, 204
The Legend of the Lone Ranger and. *See Legend of the Lone Ranger, The* (film)
press statement of, 208
restraining order of, xiii, 207, 216–17, 255
suit against, 215
"WXYZ" (Bachrach), 30
WXYZ (radio station)
early planning by, 3
first *Lone Ranger* broadcast of, 255
Moore family and, 112
original programs for, 111
Trendle purchase of, 1–2
Wyatt, Al, 123

Y
Yancey Derringer (TV serial), 139
Yates, Herbert, 6–7, 61–62, 81–82
Yellow Sky (film), 117
Yukon (radio serial), 9

Z
Zorro Rides Again (film serial), 6, 105
Zorro's Black Whip (film serial), 105
Zorro's Fighting Legion (film serial), 105